WBI DEVELOPMENT STUDIES

Knowledge, Technology, and Cluster-Based Growth in Africa

Edited by

Douglas Zhihua Zeng

The World Bank
Washington, D.C.

ISBN: 978-0-8213-7306-4
eISBN: 978-0-8213-7307-1
DOI: 10.1596/978-0-8213-7306-4

Library of Congress Cataloging-in-Publication Data

Knowledge, technology, and cluster-based growth in Africa / edited by Douglas Zhihua Zeng.
   p. cm.
  Includes bibliographical references.
    ISBN 978-0-8213-7306-4 -- ISBN 978-0-8213-7307-1 (electronic)
  1. Industrial clusters--Africa. 2. Enterprise zones--Africa. 3. Business enterprises--Africa. I. Zeng, Douglas Zhihua. II. World Bank.
   HC800.Z9D562 2007
  338.96--dc22

2007032183

Cover photo credits, clockwise from top: Curt Carnemark (floriculture), Ray Witlin (tire work), Curt Carnemark (seastress), Trevor Samson (man with flowers; and wheel repair), Eric Miller (woman in workshop), Arne Hoel (fish), Douglas Zhihua Zeng (woman and child).

Contents

Boxes

Figures

Tables

Foreword

Africa is on the move, demonstrating in recent years a significant potential for economic growth. Although the region still faces many challenges, it is also generating pockets of economic vitality in the form of enterprise clusters that are contributing to national, regional, and local productivity. These clusters, or geographically proximate groups of firms engaged in related economic activities, have enabled enterprises to access and develop capital, skills, technology, and markets and to grow and compete by diffusing knowledge and technological know-how more effectively among their members. They have been able to tap into global knowledge and technology stocks, and have encouraged product specialization by leveraging local comparative advantage, fostering production value chains, and achieving gains in efficiency. By generating employment and income, these clusters have helped lift African families out of poverty. However, in today's increasingly knowledge-intensive and competitive global economy, they also face serious challenges.

This book aims to provide an understanding of how these dynamic enterprise clusters in Africa were formed and have evolved, and how knowledge, human capital, and technology have contributed to their success. It also lays out the challenges and constraints they face while moving forward. These case studies from Ghana, Kenya, Mauritius, Nigeria, South Africa, Tanzania, and Uganda will be of interest to a broad range of development professionals. They are meant to raise awareness of this private sector growth dynamic and to help World Bank staff in the region, country governments, and donors in working with the clusters as they strive to scale up their operations. Although some broad policy implications have been drawn from the cases, they are by no means uniformly applicable across sectors and regions, and much more work is needed to make them operationally meaningful.

Rakesh Nangia
Acting Vice President
World Bank Institute

Acknowledgments

This book was financed through the generous support of the Irish Trust Fund. I would like to thank Jean-Eric Aubert, team leader of the Knowledge for Development (K4D) Program at the World Bank Institute, for his strong support and guidance throughout the case development process. I am also grateful to Bruno Laporte and Michele de Nevers who provided the organizational support for this project.

I am indebted to Professor Banji Oyeyinka from the Institute for New Technologies of the United Nations University (UNU-INTECH), who helped me organize the case studies and provided valuable advice throughout the process. I would like to thank Boladale Abiola (Aalborg University and the University of Malaya) and Nyaki Adeya (UNU-INTECH) for their substantial coordination efforts; and Aisling Quirke for her valuable assistance at the initial stage.

Thanks also go to Njeri Kinyanjui (Institute for Development Studies, University of Nairobi) and Maurice Ochieng Bolo (African Technology Policy Studies Network, Kenya) who helped organize field visits to two clusters: Kamujunji metalwork and Lake Naivasha Cut Flower in Kenya in May 2006, which greatly added value to the study.

This book also benefited from discussions with Tunc Tahsin Uyanik, Jee-Peng Tan, Shahid Yusuf, Qimiao Fan and Vadana Chandra at the World Bank, and from valuable comments by Joanna Chataway (Open University, U.K.) and Rajah Rasiah (University of Malaya, Malaysia).

Finally, I would like to acknowledge John Didier for his help in coordinating the publishing process and Steven Kennedy for providing editorial assistance.

Douglas Zhihua Zeng

1

Knowledge, Technology, and Cluster-Based Growth in Africa: Findings from 11 Case Studies of Enterprise Clusters in Africa

Douglas Zhihua Zeng

Although Africa is falling behind in today's global economic race, it holds pockets of vital economic activity—many in the form of enterprise clusters scattered across the continent's countries and industries. By clustering, enterprises are able to overcome constraints in capital, skills, technology, and markets. Enterprise clusters help their constituents grow and compete by encouraging more effective knowledge and technology diffusion and product specialization, leveraging local comparative advantage, fostering production value chains, and achieving collective efficiency. In so doing, they contribute significantly to Africa's economic growth. They provide jobs for the continent's growing population, thus enabling families not only to survive, but also to educate their children and perhaps move out of poverty. But in today's increasingly knowledge-intensive and globalized economy, these clusters also face serious challenges in the areas of technology, natural resources, infrastructure, skill acquisition, and quality control.

How were these clusters formed and how did they evolve? What are the key elements contributing to their success? How can knowledge and technology be put to work to generate economic growth even in low-income countries? Are these clusters sustainable and replicable? To gain a better understanding of these questions, the World Bank Institute organized a study of enterprise clusters in five low-income and two middle-income countries in Africa. The cases presented in the book are the work of international and local consultants (the authors of the rest of the chapters in the book) who have been working on African clusters, with evidence gathered through desk study, field visits, and surveys. This volume reports the evidence gathered, with a focus on knowledge, technology, and policy.

The Selected Clusters

Clusters are defined by two key attributes: (1) their geographic and spatial distribution, and (2) their economic sector. Porter (1990) defines a cluster as a group of firms engaged in a similar or related economic activity within the national economy. In most cases these firms are geographically close, while in others they may be more dispersed. Schmitz (1992) defines a cluster as a geographic *and* sectoral agglomeration of enterprises. While both definitions are relevant, most of the clusters we study here fall into the latter definition, as it is based on geographic proximity as well as sectoral specialization. Nadvi's (1999) collective efficiency model has four key variables that determine competitiveness in enterprise clusters—market access, labor-market pooling, intermediate input effects, and technological spillovers. The other variable in the model is what Nadvi calls *joint action*. This occurs when firms make deliberate efforts to cooperate and collaborate. The geographic proximity of clusters is assumed to facilitate joint activities initiated by the enterprises.

With regard to learning and knowledge flows, there are typically three types: formal learning (schools, training institutions, and universities); nonformal learning (structured on-the-job training); and informal learning (skills learned from family members or people in the community) (World Bank 2003). Oyelaran-Oyeyinka (2004) has also identified two types of learning: formal and nonformal (experiential learning). "Nonformal learning," he writes, "which often takes the form of learning-by-doing, is an important component of human capital, particularly in economic contexts where traditional craftsmanship, often acquired through apprenticeship, predominates." Oyelaran-Oyeyinka further notes that knowledge of production, which is tacit to a large extent, relies largely on workers' skill (know-how), although skill itself draws on "know-why" to find reasons for particular procedures or routines.

Nadvi (1997), Schmitz (1999), and Meyer-Stamer (1998) recognize that clustering offers unique opportunities to engage in a wide array of domestic links between users and producers, and between the economy's knowledge-producing sector (universities and R&D institutions) and its goods-and-services-producing sector. All of these linkages stimulate learning and innovation. Mytelka (2004) emphasizes the role of clusters in promoting the kind of interactivity that is an important stimulus of innovation, but cautions that the colocation of actors in geographic proximity does not automatically lead to interaction, learning, and innovation.

To demonstrate these points, we have chosen cases in low- and middle-income countries in East and West Africa. The sectors covered range from natural-resource-based activities, such as fishing, to high-tech industries, such as auto parts and computer manufacturing. Table 1.1 provides an overview of the case studies.

Cluster Origins

Clusters come in many forms; each has a unique development trajectory and set of organizational principles; each faces specific challenges. Two broad categories can be defined, however. In the first are clusters that originate as spontaneous agglomerations of enterprises and other related actors. The second includes clusters induced by public policies, or "constructed"; these range from "technopoles" and industrial parks to incubators and export processing zones (EPZs).

Most of the clusters we studied belong in the first category. Exceptions include the Mauritian textile and clothing cluster, which started as an EPZ, and cases where governments did take some limited action—though such efforts were not normally part of a broad plan or systemic policy. Although the 11 clusters we studied were formed in different ways and at different times, it is possible to identify some basic elements that led, in varying degrees, to their formation:

- *Natural endowments.* These are especially important for the natural-resource-based clusters, such as cut flowers in Kenya, fishing in Uganda, and wine in

Table 1.1 *Overview of 11 enterprise clusters in Africa*

Chapter	Cluster	No. of firms	Firm size (average no. of employees)	Markets	Major challenges
2	The Suame Manufacturing Cluster in Ghana	> 9,000	5–10	Domestic and limited export (West Africa)	Lack of effective dissemination of R&D results to firms; inadequate physical infrastructure
3	The Kamukunji Metalwork Cluster in Kenya	> 2,000	1–3	Domestic	Low barriers to entry and congestion of microenterprises; weak linkages with knowledge institutions; weak infrastructure support
4	The Lake Naivasha Cut Flower Cluster in Kenya	24 (large firms)	250–6,000	Domestic and export (mainly Europe)	Resource depletion and environmental pollution
5	The Nnewi Automotive Components Cluster in Nigeria	85	< 12	Domestic and limited export	Asian competition and poor public goods
6	The Otigba Computer Village Cluster in Nigeria	> 5,000	8	Domestic and export (mainly West Africa)	Lack of capital, especially long-term financing; weak infrastructure support; vulnerability to foreign exchange and import duties
7	The Mwenge Handicrafts Cluster in Tanzania	2,200	15–20	Domestic and limited export	Lack of financing; weak firm capacity; weak public institutions and infrastructure
7	The Keko Furniture Cluster in Tanzania	—	2–130	Domestic and limited export	Weak public institutions and infrastructure; lack of technological support and access to finance
8	The Lake Victoria Fishing Cluster in Uganda	17 (fishing plants)	35–200+	Domestic and export (mainly Europe)	Falling fish stock and EU quality standards
9	The Textile and Clothing Cluster in Mauritius	260	170	Domestic and international	Increasing labor costs; enhanced international competition; low productivity
10	The Wine Cluster in South Africa	> 340 (wine farms)	—	Domestic and international	Lack of effective marketing/branding strategy and expertise; financial constraints for small producers
11	The Western Cape Textile and Clothing Cluster in South Africa	327	103	Domestic and international	Increasing labor costs; enhanced international competition; lack of innovation both in product and process

Note: — Not available.
Source: Author's research.

South Africa. In the case of the Kenyan flower cluster, a favorable climate (a diverse range of temperatures and well-distributed rainfall), the availability of huge tracts of land, and fresh water resources from Lake Naivasha and underground constitute unique advantages. In the case of Uganda fishing, Lake Victoria, the biggest lake in Africa, provides very rich resources.

- *Proximity to major local markets (such as cities) and infrastructure (roads, highways, ports, airports).* This is an important factor for almost every cluster we studied. The Otigba computer village in Nigeria is located within Ikeja, the industrial capital of Lagos State and former capital of Nigeria. The Suame cluster in Ghana is located in Kumasi, the capital city of the Ashanti region and a very important and historical center for the region. In Kenya, the Kamukunji cluster is in the capital city, Nairobi, and the Lake Naivasha cluster is also near Nairobi and the Jomo Kenyatta International Airport. In Tanzania, the Mwenge cluster is located in the capital, Dar-es-Salaam, and the Keko cluster is near the Chag'ombe Road. In South Africa, the Western Cape cluster is located in the Cape Town metropolitan area.

- *Local entrepreneurs with tacit knowledge and basic skills in trading, design, or manufacturing.* In most clusters studied, the businesses were started by traders, traditional craftsman, artisans, carvers, flower farmers, and so on, who inherited their knowledge and skills through family and kinship ties or local apprenticeships. Most of them started with small and simple operations, then gradually expanded and upgraded. For example, in the cases of the Kamukunji metalwork cluster in Kenya and the Nnewi auto parts and Otigba computer clusters in Nigeria, most businesses started by trading or repairing, and then gradually evolved into assembling and manufacturing activities. In the case of the Suame manufacturing and vehicle repair cluster in Ghana, business activities evolved from manufacturing simple tools to more sophisticated metal products.

- *Market push.* As noted earlier, almost all the clusters studied are located near major local markets. In all cases, the businesses that initially formed the basis of the cluster existed to meet market needs—mostly local, except in the fishing and cut flower clusters. For example, metal products were made to meet the needs of local households and farms, and computers were produced as a result of the emerging demands of local people for information and communication technology.

- *Limited government intervention.* Although most of the clusters were created spontaneously, different levels of government intervention also contributed to the formation of some, though these interventions were normally not part of a systemic plan or policy. For example, the formation of the Mwenge cluster in Tanzania and Suame cluster in Ghana were facilitated by government orders to move scattered or unorganized business activities into their current locations for the purpose of spatial planning or "keeping the city clean." The establishment of the Mauritian textile and clothing cluster began with an EPZ in the 1970s, when the very first textile and clothing firms began to operate.

How Do the Clusters Develop and Succeed?

Clusters survive and succeed mainly because they are able to upgrade the diversity and sophistication of their business activities to achieve greater productivity.

They accomplish this by building up a supply-production-distribution value chain; acquiring, disseminating, and adapting knowledge and technology (both domestic and foreign); building a relatively educated labor force; achieving collective efficiency through joint actions and cooperation; and gaining support from national and local governments, institutes, and in some cases, international bodies (such as the European Union, World Bank, and United Nations). We will discuss these efforts in more detail later.

Efficiency Gains through Cluster-Based Business Value Chains

When a cluster achieves a certain economy of scale and visibility, it begins to exert a strong pull on suppliers, marketers, distributors, users, and even financiers and providers of communication and business services. Along with them come more producers and manufacturers to take advantage of easy access to a mass clientele, as well as the cluster's interfirm synergies, knowledge network, and an infrastructure that includes many shared facilities and services (some of which, like warehouses, are provided by the government and donors). Such efficiency gains are demonstrated by the Otigba computer village, Lake Victoria fishing, Suame metalwork, and other clusters, although the components of the value chain are somewhat different in each. These value chains reduce transaction costs and greatly enhance the productivity and efficiency of all the business activities in the cluster.

Knowledge and Technology Acquisition, Adaptation, and Dissemination

Generally speaking, *knowledge* is an awareness of facts, methods, and issues related to an object or phenomenon; *technology* refers to the methods and tools needed to do things. In today's economy, knowledge and technology have become the key drivers of economic growth and firm competitiveness. This is true even for less knowledge- and technology-intensive sectors. All the cases included in our study show that effective knowledge and technology acquisition, adaptation (including some innovation), and dissemination are among the critical factors of success. The major means of engaging in these activities are the following:

KNOWLEDGE NETWORK AND INTERFIRM LINKS A knowledge network is defined as a structure of interlinked actors that, in the process of innovation, facilitate further learning in firms and institutions. Interfirm links can be both horizontal and vertical. In broad terms, there are several forms of networks and interfirm links, including: subcontracting, market links with customers and suppliers, informal and formal collaborations (joint ventures, franchises), membership in professional and trade associations (to be discussed later), and the movement of skilled staff from one firm to another (Oyelaran-Oyeyinka 2001). All of these forms of networks or interfirm links exist in the cases we studied, though to different degrees.

In the case of the Suame cluster, subcontracting is prevalent, and the contracting firms often provide some technical assistance to help suppliers achieve higher-quality standards and technical specifications. In the case of the Kenyan flower cluster, subcontracting is necessary for small farms that fail to get accreditation or certification to sell directly to export markets (mainly in Europe). Such farms need to sell through larger farms. Other reasons for subcontracting include areas of high cost associated with the flower business, such as freight and marketing, and the failure

Table 1.2. *Sources of new ideas in the Mwenge handicrafts cluster*

Source	Percentage of firms citing link as primary source
Specification by clients	45
Catalogs and magazines	24
Visiting domestic trade fairs	15
Hired designers	10
Visiting trade fairs abroad	4
Others	2

Source: Chapter 7.

of large farms to grow particular varieties in demand either because of unfavorable climatic conditions or because the demand is short-term and does not justify investment in extra operational costs. In both clusters in Tanzania, interfirm links are manifest in subcontracting, collaboration, and mechanisms for information exchange and dissemination. Poaching of labor, labor mobility, and other forms of interfirm links can be found in Lake Naivasha, Mwenge, and all other clusters. In addition, customers and clients are important sources of innovation—as observed in the Mwenge and Kamukunji clusters. In Mwenge, clients are the most significant sources of innovation and new designs (table 1.2).

Networks and linkages greatly enhance firms' ability to improve production, process innovation, and overall competitiveness.

Tapping into foreign knowledge and technology With the knowledge revolution, there is a vast stock of knowledge and technology available in the global market, especially in developed countries. Tapping into that global stock, adapting it, and using it for local economic growth are becoming increasingly important for developing countries.

Although in most clusters, firms acquire knowledge and technology domestically, there are a few cases where the technology and know-how are acquired from abroad, mainly through cooperative production agreements, franchising, licensing, reverse engineering, and imitation. Such cases include the Otigba computer village, Nnewi auto parts, Kamukunji metalwork, and Mauritian textile and clothing clusters. In Otigba, computer hardware is imported from China, Malaysia, and Dubai, and technical and production channels have been established with firms in these countries. Through reverse engineering, local technicians have acquired process technology needed for computer assembly. In Nnewi, practically all the firms obtained their technology from Taiwan (China). They also rely on Taiwan for machinery, equipment, and skills. In Kamukunji, local technology input is low and has to be imported from countries such as China, India, Republic of Korea, and Pakistan. Local entrepreneurs observe new products, study them, and design ways of producing similar products or others that can serve the same function. To facilitate product importation, the government waives the duty on basic engineering machines. In the Mauritian textile and clothing cluster, direct foreign investments from Taiwan in the 1980s and Hong Kong (China) in the 1990s played an important role in transferring technology and know-how. Foreign direct investment from Taiwan also contributed significantly to the South African textile and clothing cluster.

LEARNING AND TRAINING Various modes of learning and training activities—formal, nonformal, and informal—are important means of acquiring and disseminating knowledge and technology in the clusters. In general, the following modes of learning and training can be identified: (a) apprenticeship; (b) on-site training at suppliers' factories; (c) on-the-job training; (d) expert contracting; (e) support mechanisms provided by public institutions; (f) learning through transaction with local and external agents; and (g) learning by doing in the areas of production and maintenance. In most clusters, informal learning, such as apprenticeship, learning by doing, and learning through transactions, is quite prevalent. On-the-job training, on-site training, and expert contracting are also available in most clusters, especially those that are related to manufacturing. This is because manufacturing clusters, such as Nnewi and Kamukunji, have higher technology intensity than clusters based on natural resources or assembly. In the case of Nnewi, foreign experts are hired to provide training, and Nigerian technicians are also sent to suppliers' factories to be trained. In the two clusters in Tanzania, a survey shows that 80 percent of workers obtained skills from within their firms (on-the-job or in-house training); the remaining 20 percent obtained skills through previous employment, organized workshops, vocational training, or similar means. In the South African wine cluster, most of the established producers are actively engaged in exchanging production knowledge through viniculture forums, root stock associations, and Elsenburg—a training institute with vineyards and a cellar. Training organized or provided by public institutions is also available in most clusters.

UNIVERSITIES AND TECHNOLOGY INSTITUTES Universities and technology institutes play a crucial role in the creation, dissemination, and application of knowledge and technology. But in the development of the African clusters we studied, such as the Otigba, Kamukunji, and Tanzanian clusters, the role of universities and technology institutes has been minimal, with few exceptions. In some cases, they provided qualified technical and engineering graduates, and, in a few cases, valuable technological and technical assistance. In the case of Suame, the Suame Intermediate Technology Transfer Unit, part of the Technology Consultancy Center at the Kwame Nkrumah University of Science and Technology, and the National Vocational Training Institute provided substantial technological assistance that was very important to the cluster's upgrade and expansion. In the Kenyan flower cluster, the National Horticultural Research Center and several universities offered training programs in horticulture. In the Ugandan fishing cluster, universities also provided training in fisheries and aquaculture. In the South African wine cluster, the Wine Industry Network for Expertise and Technology played an important role in coordinating research, technology transfer, and training.

Pooling of Relatively Educated Entrepreneurs and Workers

An educated, skilled labor force is the core of firm innovation and competitiveness. Although, in general, Africa suffers from a shortage of skilled human capital, the clusters we studied benefit from a relatively educated labor force—though their education levels are still low compared with their counterparts in more developed countries. In a few clusters, such as the Otigba cluster in Nigeria, there is a high concentration of well-educated workers. This is one of the important reasons why the clusters can perform better than the rest of the economy.

Table 1.3. *Education levels of entrepreneurs in selected clusters*
Percent

Level of education	Mwenge	Keko	Suame	Nnewi	Western Cape
Primary or below	38.9	25	75	42.9	82.5 (semi- and unskilled)
Junior secondary	22.2	50	23	40.8	13.1 (skilled)
Senior secondary	16.7	25			
Tertiary	22.2	0	2	16.3	4.4 (highly skilled)
Total	100.0	100.0	100.0	100.0	100.0

Source: Chapters 2, 5, 7, and 11.
Note: The ways of assessing education level are different. In the Tanzanian clusters (first two columns), secondary education is from 8 to 13 years and tertiary is 14 years and above, while in Suame, secondary is 9–12 years, and tertiary is 13 years and above.

Although data on the entire labor force in the clusters are not available, some data (including surveys) are available about cluster entrepreneurs. Based on the data provided in the case studies, in some clusters, the majority of entrepreneurs have at least a primary school education; a significant number have completed junior secondary school (20–50 percent) and senior secondary school (17–25 percent) (table 1.3). In the Nnewi cluster, 40.8 percent of the surveyed entrepreneurs have a secondary school education, and 28.8 percent a technical education; 16.3 percent of the entrepreneurs hold university degrees.[1] In Otigba, about 55–60 percent of the entrepreneurs are university graduates, and there is an uncommon presence of highly skilled and educated graduates in electronics, computer sciences, and related disciplines. This contrasts sharply with the Suame cluster in Ghana, where 75 percent of the entrepreneurs received no more than a primary education, and only 2 percent obtained higher education. Meanwhile, more college graduates with advanced degrees continue to join various clusters, becoming important catalysts of continued growth.

Governmental and Institutional Support

The role of governments and public institutions differ from cluster to cluster. In some clusters, governmental involvement is minimal (such as in Kamukunji, where the major governmental initiative was to provide sheds); in others, the government provided some facilitation or played a significant role. In general, government interventions are manifested in the following areas: defining and enforcing sectoral policies, regulations, and standards; creating a special agency or organization to promote, coordinate, and facilitate cluster development; establishing various public institutions (such as councils, incubators, technology centers, and institutes) to provide technological and technical support, training (in technology, business, entrepreneurship, management), and capacity development; providing incentives

---

1. These data are drawn from a 2005 survey and represent a significant improvement in the educational attainment of owners. New owners of businesses with university degrees have begun to enter into the cluster, in contrast with a 1997 study, which reported only one person with a tertiary education degree. See Chapter 5.

such as tax holidays, special funds, duty-free provisions, and cheap land to promote technology imports and enterprise development; promoting alliances and partnerships among local firms and with foreign firms through joint ventures and strategic alliances (in the case of Otigba); and providing infrastructure such as roads, water, power, ports, warehouses, information technology (IT) facilities, and so on. These initiatives are present in varying degrees in different clusters; in some, most initiatives exist while, in others, only one or two are present.

In the Kenyan cut flower cluster, the government played a very positive and instrumental role. The government of Kenya recognized the importance of horticulture in the national economy as early as 1966 and committed to promoting its growth. In 1967, horticulture was declared a special crop and accorded priority in the government's agenda. The government created the Horticultural Crops Development Authority (HCDA) to develop, promote, coordinate, and facilitate the horticultural industry in Kenya. Meanwhile, it enacted legislation to protect intellectual property rights and enforce quality standards, and set up promotion schemes such as manufacturing under bond, export compensation, and export promotion zones to support horticultural exports. Otherwise, the government's direct involvement in the subsector has been minimal, limited mainly to issuing export licenses through HCDA. It has not interfered in the marketing or distribution of the crops, leaving these functions to the private sector. Such an enabling environment and the government's subsequent hands-off approach have encouraged very strong and robust private sector participation in the cut flower industry.

Some of these clusters benefited from the support of international organizations. For example, the World Bank has been involved in Kamukunji activities, especially in the areas of skill and technology development. The cluster also benefited from skill development programs sponsored by the United Nations Development Programme and United Nations Industrial Development Organization. In Suame, the World Bank organized short-term, hands-on training for auto mechanics and auto electricians.

Joint Action and Cooperation

Because of the small size of most cluster enterprises, it is very important for firms to establish joint organizations and cooperate to protect their common interests; exchange information and ideas; form synergies and interfirm links; provide technical, marketing, and policy services; increase collective bargaining powers; and survive in the face of fierce competition. Such collective gains are normally obtained through various industrial and professional associations. In almost all the clusters, one finds various associations. These play different roles in each cluster. For example, in the Tanzanian clusters, associations help firms voice their concerns, provide valuable sources of information, and offer technological advice. In Suame, associations are mainly concerned with social welfare issues. In the case of the Kenyan cut flower cluster, associations' objectives range from lobbying for policy support and environmental conservation to maintaining standards and facilitating corporate social responsibility. The Kenya Flower Council and the Fresh Produce Exporters Association are the key industrial associations, the objectives of which include maintaining standards, facilitating market access, and gathering market intelligence for members. In the South African wine cluster, Wines of South Africa plays an important role in marketing South African wines internationally.

Are Africa's Clusters Sustainable and Susceptible to Scaling Up?

Clustering does contribute to the success and growth of a specific sector by offering various advantages not available outside the clusters. However, while African clusters have achieved some success, they also face serious challenges and constraints. Their growth and sustainability in the long run will, to a large extent, depend on how they can cope with these challenges. If they are successful, they could be expanded and scaled up—otherwise, their future may be uncertain.

Challenges of the Knowledge Revolution and Increasing Global Competition

With today's global knowledge revolution, firms and industries are rapidly becoming more knowledge- and technology-intensive; accordingly, their means of production and operation are also becoming increasingly knowledge-based. This requires an increasingly intensive acquisition, adaptation, and use of knowledge and technology throughout the sector to enhance productivity and efficiency (Zeng and Wang 2007). While there are successful clusters (including those we studied), most confine their operations to Africa (the exceptions are cut flowers, fishing, wine, and textiles and clothing) or remain domestic enclaves. The firms in the clusters are small and, in general, lack access to capital, skills, and technologies; for the most part, they demonstrate limited innovation. Although the clusters in South Africa and Mauritius are relatively strong and compete internationally, they are losing ground owing to rising labor costs, falling productivity, and lack of innovation—and the possible change of criteria or eventual phaseout of the EU's Everything But Arms trade initiative and the U.S. African Growth and Opportunity Act (AGOA) after 2015, would make it harder for them to compete. As the market becomes more globalized, the firms in these clusters face more competition from Asian countries, such as China, India, and Vietnam. Surviving that competition will pose a big challenge.

Lack of a Critical Mass of Skills and Talent

Although the clusters we studied boast a relatively educated labor force, their overall educational level is still low compared with clusters elsewhere in the world. In a market that allows firms to produce and sell relatively unsophisticated products, higher skill levels may not be exploited in the short term. However, to sustain competitiveness, firms have to gradually move up the value chain and become more innovative. This requires having more talented technicians and engineers, who currently are not available in most clusters. For example, the Suame cluster already faces an oversupply of new entrants due to low entry barriers and a low technology level. To survive global competition, firms have to be more innovative.

Weak Links Between Businesses and Knowledge Institutions

Based on our studies, institutions of higher education are providing some skilled personnel, but, in general, their contribution is limited owing to poor-quality education and a mismatch between skill supply and market demand. For example, in Kamukunji even new graduates from national institutes of technology, national polytechnics, and universities were not viewed as sources of knowledge in the cluster. Except in a few cases, universities and technology institutes are not deeply involved in firms' technology and innovation activities. This may be traceable to weak demand from the private sector and the limited capacity of the universities and technology institutes. In Otigba, for example, it is thought that the collective IT capabilities in the cluster are much higher than those found in most IT-focused faculties in Nigerian universities and polytechnics.

Weak Governmental and Institutional Support

As noted earlier, the level of governmental involvement varies across the clusters. In Kenya's cut flower cluster and in the textile and wine clusters in South Africa and Mauritius, the government has played a very positive and conducive role. However, in most cases, the role of the government and support from public institutions are inadequate. Beyond providing some basic infrastructure and training, the government needs to build a conducive business environment. This is not just an issue of defining policies, but of implementing them. Based on a survey in the Nnewi cluster, most firms perceived governmental support as weak (table 1.4).

Resource Depletion and Failure to Meet International Standards

These challenges mainly apply to the natural-resource-based clusters in our study, notably Kenya's cut flower cluster and Uganda's fishing cluster. In the case of Kenya's cut flower industry, overdrawing water from Lake Naivasha for irrigation purposes threatens the lake's existence. In some places, the water in the lake has retreated by more than 700 meters from its position before the advent of large-scale irrigation. In addition, an accumulation of agrochemical effluents, especially nitrates, threatens aquatic life. Fish stocks have been reduced, and diseases and pests are on the rise. Meanwhile, the Ugandan fishing cluster has faced problems in meeting EU standards for safety and quality. Beginning in 1997, the European Union imposed and enforced a set of sanitary and phytosanitary standards on Uganda's fish exports. Failure to meet the standards led to a conditional ban on one of Uganda's most important exports and a crisis in the fish-processing and export industry. After both the public and private sectors made a joint rescue effort, focusing on process improvement, access to the EU market was restored. Uganda has not yet succeeded, however, in translating its successful response to the EU fish ban into a cohesive, proactive development process. In the medium- and long-term, a focus on

Table 1.4. Firms' perception of government support in Nnewi cluster
Percentage of firms citing given level of support

Strength of support	Area of support						
	Innovation	Available skilled manpower	Public university support	R&D	Intellectual property protection	IT support	Venture capital
Weak	89.8	77.1	89.4	93.8	87.5	91.1	95.7
Good	8.2	16.7	10.6	6.3	10.4	8.9	2.1
Strong	2.0	6.3	0.0	0.0	2.1	0.0	2.1
Total	100.0	100.0	100.0	100.0	100.0	100.0	100.0

Source: Chapter 5.

technological capability and innovation could lead to systemic product upgrades, providing a basis for the sustained competitiveness of Uganda's fish exports.

From the above analyses we can see that the challenges facing Africa's clusters are still enormous, though varied across sectors. Clusters' future sustainability and susceptibility to scaling up depends, to a great extent, on how successfully the clusters can overcome these challenges. For resource-based clusters, even those that are currently successful and function in international markets, a failure to solve the challenges of resource depletion and product upgrading will place long-term sustainability in doubt. The survival of technology-based clusters depends on how effectively the clusters can absorb and apply new technologies and adopt advanced knowledge-management practices to improve their overall competitiveness.

Clusters are important pockets of economic vitality. For them to become truly sustainable and scalable, the government has a vital and multifaceted role to play. In addition to providing leadership and coordination, the public sector needs to establish a favorable regulatory and incentive-based environment, facilitating innovation and the acquisition of knowledge and technology. It should also provide high-quality public goods from which the private sector can benefit.

Some Policy Implications

Several policy implications can be drawn from our studies, but these are by no means uniformly applicable to all clusters in Africa. Some clusters are of medium size, with a potential for considerable capability acquisition. Most firms in the clusters are owned by individuals who are resourceful and educated, with a complement of relatively skilled workers. Firm dynamism is usually limited by market type and size. To meet the needs of clusters' diverse contexts and industries, policy design and implementation must be carefully considered and well planned. Government measures might include efforts to:

- *Encourage further knowledge acquisition, adaptation, and dissemination.* Based on clusters' current knowledge networks and interfirm links, collaboration should be encouraged, especially with foreign companies. To tap into foreign technologies and apply them in a local context is crucial for improving clusters' competitiveness. Nnewi's close link with Taiwan is an example of such collaboration. In addition to training and technical assistance collaborations, medium and large enterprises should also be encouraged to engage in R&D and innovation.
- *Strengthen educational institutions and technology institutes and their link with the business sector.* Technology institutes and universities (both public and private) should be encouraged to become more attuned to industry needs. They should reach out to firms with offers to provide technology support (such as R&D and technology brokering) and technical assistance. Policy incentives can be designed to encourage joint research, contracted services, and other types of collaboration. Universities must provide more skilled graduates to meet market demands. To accomplish this, some educational reforms, including in curricula and overall pedagogy, are necessary.
- *Establish and enforce a business-conducive institutional plan, including clear regulations, standards, and quality assurance mechanisms.* These are important for building an enabling business environment, encouraging innovation, and delivering quality products. In defining and carrying out such a plan, a close public–

private partnership is very important. Many tasks can be done in collaboration with trade and professional associations, which are present in almost every cluster. In some cases, the function of associations needs to be strengthened.

- *Strengthen and upgrade skill training.* In most clusters studied, skill levels are low, as are education levels, with a majority of the labor force having completed only primary school or junior secondary school. To enhance productivity and cope with increasing international competition, African firms need to upgrade the skill level of their labor force. This is also essential for product and process innovation, the key factors in promoting firms' long-term survival. Improving skill levels must be done through close collaboration with universities, technology institutes, and training organizations. The focus should be not just on production technology, but on business management, marketing, branding, and packaging.

- *Provide sound infrastructure.* Although governments have been involved in providing basic infrastructure to some clusters, the effort is insufficient. Firms are constrained by poor public goods delivery—water, power supply, phone lines, and so on. For example, in the Nnewi cluster, 98 percent of firms claim that they have to spend a nontrivial percentage—in some cases up to 40 percent—of their total investment on private power generation and other utilities. This issue has to be addressed by the government.

- *In the long run, promote greater consumer purchasing power.* Firms grow when markets expand and, more importantly, when income levels are able to sustain high-quality consumer goods. Relevant policies should be seen in the light of enterprise promotion, leading to the evolution of higher levels of subcontracting and specialization.

References

Meyer-Stamer, Jörg. 1998. "Path Dependence in Regional Development: Persistence and Change in Three Industrial Clusters in Santa Catarina, Brazil." *World Development*, 26(8): 1495–1511.

Mytelka, L. 2004. "From Clusters to Innovation Systems in Traditional Industries." In B. L. M. Mwamila, L. Trojer, B. Diyamett and A. K. Temu, eds., *Innovation Systems and Innovative Clusters in Africa*. Proceedings of a regional conference, Bagamoyo, Tanzania.

Nadvi, K. 1997. "The Cutting Edge: Collective Efficiency and International Competitiveness in Pakistan." IDS Discussion Paper No. 360. IDS, Brighton.

———. 1999. "Collective Efficiency and Collective Failure: The Response of the Sialkot Surgical Instruments Cluster to Global Quality Pressures." *World Development* 27(9).

Oyelaran-Oyeyinka, Banji. 2001. "Networks and Linkages in African Manufacturing Cluster: A Nigerian Case Study." Discussion paper, United Nations University.

———. 2004. "Building Innovative Clusters—The Role of Learning and Local Capabilities." In B. L. M. Mwamila, L. Trojer, B. Diyamett and A. K. Temu, eds., *Innovation Systems and Innovative Clusters in Africa*. Proceedings of a regional conference, Bagamoyo, Tanzania.

Porter, Michael. 1990. *The Competitive Advantage of Nations*. New York: Basic Books.

Schmitz, H. 1992. "On the Clustering of Small Firms." *IDS Bulletin*, 23(3): 64–69.

World Bank. 2003. "Lifelong Learning in the Global Knowledge Economy: Challenges for Developing Countries." Human Development Network, Washington, D.C.

Zeng, Douglas Zhihua, S. Wang. 2007. "China and the Knowledge Economy: Challenges and Opportunities." World Bank Policy Research Working Paper 4223, Washington, D.C.

2

The Suame Manufacturing Cluster in Ghana

Catherine Nyaki Adeya

The Suame manufacturing cluster in Kumasi—also known as *Suame Magazine* because the site, established as an armory, once housed a military magazine—has a long history of craftsmanship.[1] As early as the 1920s, emerging artisans and craftsmen of Kumasi, the capital of the Ashanti region, accumulated excellent skills and knowledge in blacksmithing, goldsmith, and the making of the brass artifacts that were the prevalent craft in Kumasi at the time. Enterprises began clustering around former armories in Kumasi as early as 1935. Most started as family businesses; when vehicle repair became lucrative, craftsmen with similar skills grouped together.[2]

The Suame cluster site was created in the 1950s and 1960s when its entrepreneurs were relocated from the Kumasi city center by the Kumasi City Council. A key turning point in the cluster's history occurred in the mid-1970s, when the government placed tight restrictions on the importation of new vehicles and parts (Dawson 1988). This crippled large enterprises, which were capital-intensive and relied on imports; small enterprises filled the gap by improvising the spare parts that had been previously imported. Though the importation of spare parts and even whole vehicles resumed under the Economic Recovery Program in the 1980s, large enterprises did not regain their previous dominance.

The land where the Suame cluster is located is zoned for administrative purposes, but plots within the zones are not well demarcated. This is mainly due to the haphazard construction of temporary workshops by "squatter artisans." For the purposes of spatial planning and land administration, the magazines in Kumasi (such as Asafo, Ahinsan, Krofrom, Sofoline, and Suame) were categorized into 21 zones. Suame Magazine (1.8 km by 0.3 km) contains zones 1–7, 11–13, and 18–19. The inconsistency in numbering is due to the rapid emergence of other magazines in Kumasi.

The growing population of Suame Magazine requires the attention of the government and other stakeholders. The cluster needs new physical infrastructure

---

1. In northern Ghana, similar groupings have also adopted the term *magazine* as part of their names, while in the south they are referred to as *Kokompes*, after a suburb in Accra popularly known for activities similar to those of Suame.
2. This chapter is drawn come from a study coordinated by Nyaki Adeya (2001) while she was a research fellow at UNU-INTECH in Maastricht. Now a private consultant based in Nairobi, Dr. Adeya revised her study for this volume.

Figure 2.1. *Population growth of Suame Magazine*

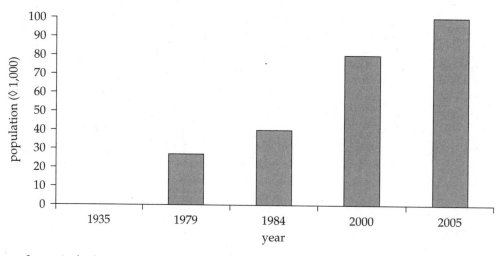

Source: Author's research.

(telecommunications, electricity, water, access roads, and health posts), while existing infrastructure must be expanded to support spillover from small workshops. In 1984, more than 40,000 people were working in Suame; that number doubled by 2000 (Obeng 2002). According to surveys conducted in the 1980s by the Technology Consultancy Centre (TCC) of the Kwame Nkrumah University of Science and Technology (KNUST), the labor force of Suame Magazine was expected to grow at approximately 8 percent per annum through the 1990s (Ghana Statistical Service 2002). This exceeds the region's average urban migration rate of 4.5 percent, and is composed mostly of youth, who come in search of better learning opportunities and employment. Figure 2.1 illustrates the estimated population growth of Suame Magazine between 1935 and 2005.

Economic Context

The Suame cluster is dominated by micro and small enterprises (MSEs). On average, enterprises have five workers; more sophisticated manufacturing workshops generally have 7 to 10. Their main activities can be categorized as manufacturing, vehicle repair, metalworking, and the sale of engineering materials, spare automobile parts, and food. Communication centers are playing an increasingly important role in cluster activities. The cluster's major products and services are listed in table 2.1.

Outside the cluster location in Kumasi, there is intense competition among small, medium, and large vehicle repair companies. Most enterprises seem to wait for business to come to them; very few try to create and maintain working relationships with, for example, large firms that do not have their own garage facilities (Dawson 1988).

The adoption of both basic technologies and relatively complex machinery, such as tool-making machines, has raised the engineering capability of firms. The stock of machine tools in Suame Magazine expanded rapidly between 1971 and 1986 with the assistance of the Suame Intermediate Technology Transfer Unit (ITTU) of

Table 2.1. *Products and services of the Suame cluster*

Major sectors	Products and services
Manufacturing	Food-processing equipment and farm implements; cooking stoves and utensils; foundry products
Vehicle repair and maintenance	Engine overhauling; auto electric works; vehicle interior upholstery; auto body work (straightening and painting)
Metalworking	Metal fabrication and plant construction; angle irons, channel iron bars
Sales of engineering materials and accessories	Sheet metal, bars, iron rods, steel sections, hand tools, fasteners, electric motors, pumps
Sales of spare automobile parts	Second-hand engines and parts; car-decorating materials
Sales of food	Foods and beverages of all kinds
Communication and business centers	Telephone and fax services, photocopying, computer typesetting; Internet and e-mail services; sales of mobile phone cards and videocassettes; barbering and sales of soft drinks

Source: Adeya 2001.

the TCC in Kumasi (Powell 1986). The ITTU was established by the government of Ghana to raise the technical competence of the cluster by providing technology advisory services and machinery upgrades. The result was increased competition among enterprises, for example, in the manufacture of corn milling machines, planters, and ploughs. However, trade in engineering materials and spare parts is currently more profitable than manufacture and repair work. One advantage the manufacturing MSEs have over other sectors, such as predominantly import-dependent retail, is their ability to create downstream industries through the production of machinery and equipment using locally available human and material resources.

External Economies

The cluster's concentration of vehicle-repair enterprises in one location brings together customers and repairers—and may explain the lack of aggressive marketing. Labor market pooling is a positive feature of Suame. McCormick (1998) found two types of labor in the cluster: workers mainly apprenticed to small enterprises (the author does not discuss their skill levels in detail, but it is assumed that these are not high), and workers with higher-level technical skills gained in large-enterprise apprenticeships and technical training institutes. The presence of the second group has enabled the cluster to produce some items that can compete favorably with imports. Suame's vehicle mechanics manage to achieve greater efficiency than those of many other small-enterprise clusters because they subcontract a great deal among themselves, enabling the entire grouping of enterprises to achieve basic economies of scale.

The market of the Suame cluster includes the government, private firms, and individuals. The products of its enterprises are also popular in other West African countries such as Burkina Faso, Côte d'Ivoire, Mali, and Togo. The market for vehicle repair benefits from the cluster's location on the main road linking two capital cities, Accra (Ghana) and Abidjan (Côte d'Ivoire).

Joint Action

Only Suame's metal product engineering workshops are reported to have positive bilateral links with site associations that represent diverse interests. (Site associations are geographically based groups representing the different crafts and skills-based groups within the cluster.) There are also some vertical links, mainly intermediary, between engineering workshop enterprises and the government (McCormick 1998). Such links could be further facilitated and strengthened by information and communications technology (ICT), for example, to create a database of the expertise and locations of various enterprises so that firms wishing to subcontract could easily contact appropriate firms instead of spending time searching for potential subcontractors, which has been common in Suame. At present many contracts are gained through personal referrals (mostly through friends and family), which may leave out some firms that could potentially benefit but lack the right connections.

There are many associations in Suame, but their activities are derailed by both internal and external problems. Many workers end up establishing their own associations when they are dissatisfied with existing ones. This has led to a proliferation of associations, most of which focus on social welfare issues and are rarely concerned with supply-side matters, markets, and technology. This slows down MSE development because the associations are not effectively grouping enterprises with similar interests so that they can lobby for better services, such as ICT-related infrastructure.

Properly conceived and run, associations can influence policy relevant to MSEs and serve as forums for sharing information vital to improved business practices. In 1983 the Ministry of Industries created the Suame Garages Association to act as a communication channel between the government and cluster artisans, as well as to deliver assistance programs. The association selected enterprises to benefit from a World Bank program, as well as artisans to take part in other training programs—but not without controversy. Dawson (1988) and McCormick (1998) surmise that the controversy had two main sources: First, the association represented too many enterprises of varying sizes and activity types; second, because it was a creation of the government its legitimacy was questioned by both existing and potential members.

Other associations in Suame include:

Magazine Mechanical Association. About 98 percent of the entrepreneurs in Suame belong to the Magazine Mechanical Association, established in 1957. Initially, its main objectives were to assist bereaved members in organizing funerals and settling land disputes. Now the association controls more than 800 building plots in the lowland areas of Suame Magazine. It has approximately 10,000 members, most of them vehicle mechanics. The daily activities of its secretariat include meetings and consultations on member problems and tax and levy collection. The association has a permanent building in the cluster.

Ghana National Association of Garages. Formed in the 1980s, the association has offices in several parts of Ghana, including a regional secretariat in the Suame cluster. The association controls approximately 1,000 building plots in the upland areas of Suame Magazine. Its main objectives are land administration and the general welfare of young vehicle mechanics.

Association of Micro and Small Metal Industries. In the 1990s, clients of the Suame ITTU formed the Association of Micro and Small Metal Industries to address the problems of the metal manufacturing subsector. Approximately 60 members, most of them workshop owners, meet at the Suame ITTU. In 1998, the Suame ITTU recommended six members of the association to the GRATIS Foundation for working capital loans and machine tool purchases to expand their businesses. The association is working with the TCC and the GRATIS Foundation to establish a national network.

Magazine Spare Parts Dealers Association. This association is composed of middle-class business people mainly involved in the importation of spare parts for automobile repair. By virtue of their business, spare parts dealers are intensive users of communication facilities. In shops where there are no communication devices, workers use the services of the communication centers in and around the Suame cluster.

Engine Reborers Association. This association is dedicated to the general welfare of those engaged in reboring and resleeving worn-out vehicle engines. There are about 30 members located within the cluster.

Magazine Caterers Association. Members are mostly women who sell food within the cluster. For the most part, this association is a social group that organizes marriages, funerals, and other social activities.

There are other associations in the formative stage in Suame Magazine; these include the Magazine Auto-mechanics Association, Foundry Association, and Scrap Dealers Association. In addition, there are a number of support institutions involved in programs to reduce poverty and train youth in employable skills. Over the last decade there has been significant progress in the training and support given to MSEs, but these efforts are still limited in their coverage.

Knowledge and Technology within the Cluster

The Suame cluster has some of the most mature MSEs in Africa (Adeya 2001). McCormick (1998) reported that the Suame cluster had approximately 9,000 engineering enterprises (4,000 in metal product manufacturing and 5,000 in vehicle repair). Although McCormick's study offers valuable information on cluster enterprises, it underestimates the number of enterprises in the Suame cluster since it does not consider trading enterprises. Our research shows that trading enterprises are major actors that play a complementary role in the sale and supply of engineering materials, tools, and spare parts to metal workers and vehicle repairers.

The majority of workers surveyed (92 percent) completed either only primary school (69 percent) or secondary (23 percent) (table 2.2). No respondent had a tertiary education; only 4 percent had had no formal schooling. A few of the respondents admitted that they were school dropouts. However, this did not seem to affect their success, as they are among the successful entrepreneurs within the cluster.

A few (2 percent) of the respondents undertook professional courses or vocational training after basic schooling. Many respondents were introduced into the profession by their relatives and kin. They have known no other business since childhood. Many aspired to own a store or enterprise within the cluster, and acquiring a formal education was not a priority in their lives (Grieco, Apt, and Turner 1996; King 1999). Some found their way into the cluster because their parents could not afford to pay for formal education.

Table 2.2. Education levels of respondents

| | Gender | | | | | |
| | Male | | Female | | Total | |
Level of education	Frequency	Percent	Frequency	Percent	Frequency	Percent
None (illiterate)	4	5	0	0	4	5
None (literate)	1	1	0	0	1	1
4–8 yrs	52	58	10	10	62	69
9–12 yrs	18	20	3	3	21	23
13 yrs	2	2	0	0	2	2
Total	77	86	13	14	90	100

Source: Author 2001.

A study conducted by Adeya (2001) identified worker skill types and how they were acquired. The objective was to understand the different modes of learning in firms and how enterprises acquire skills and capabilities through learning (table 2.3). Apprenticeship is the dominant mode of skill acquisition, used by 74 percent of workers.

Apart from the training provided by the Suame ITTU and the National Vocational and Technical Institute, formal training is rare within the cluster. Many enterprise owners, especially those in vehicle servicing and trading, are trained on the job or through apprenticeship. Sometimes trainees are family members. Ninety percent of the respondents said they have the skills necessary to work in their enterprises, and only 10 percent felt they needed to acquire more. Seventy-four percent of respondents acquired their skills on the job, 16 percent gained their skills through formal learning, while 8 percent acquired skills through self-coaching and teaching (table 2.3).

Of business owners and managers, 69 percent of 90 respondents said that their employees are skilled, while just 4 percent responded negatively; 27 percent had no employees. It is possible that some who responded positively do not have permanent employees, but instead have apprentices who work with them to gain further experience or to accumulate enough resources to establish new enterprises.

The government of Ghana recognizes the need to upgrade the knowledge and skills of the artisans in Suame. While there is an evident pool of basic skills, research has identified that in order to function effectively in a competitive envi-

Table 2.3. Primary sources of acquired skills

Source of skills acquired	Frequency	Percent
Formal learning institutions	13	16
Brought up on the job or in the business	1	1
On-the-job training (apprenticeship)	61	74
Previous formal employment	1	1
Self-learning/apprenticeship	7	8
Total	82	100

Source: Adeya 2001.

ronment, a knowledge of basic engineering drawing (manual and computer aided) and the use of modern tools and equipment is required.

The Suame ITTU and the National Vocational Training Institute are the two institutions established within the cluster to provide training in basic skills and new technologies and support the certification of apprentice training. In the past, the World Bank organized short-term, hands-on training for the auto mechanics and auto electricians of Suame through the Kumasi Technical Institute, but this program stalled due to lack of sustained funding (Velenchik 1995). Most programs tend to focus assistance in the areas of finance, manpower training, technology transfer, and improved business practices.

Policy Incentives

In an effort to develop small-scale enterprises, the government of Ghana established institutions to ensure the growth and expansion of MSEs. These institutions have collaborated with the MSEs of Suame, and continue to do so in the areas of technology development and transfer, vocational and apprentice training, business management and entrepreneurship training, working capital and hire-purchase loans, women's enterprise development, business-assistance funds, and marketing. Some notable institutions (several of which have already been introduced) are:

- Council for Scientific and Industrial Research
- Suame Intermediate Technology Transfer Unit
- National Vocational Training Institute
- Ghana Regional Appropriate Technology Industrial Service (GRATIS Foundation)
- National Board for Small-Scale Industries
- Technology Consultancy Center
- Association of Small-Scale Industries
- Association of Ghana Industries
- Private Enterprise Foundation
- Intermediate Technology Ghana

The Council for Scientific and Industrial Research is responsible for the coordination of most of Ghana's research institutes. It has several R&D departments thtat assess the development of new technologies and machines for agriculture and water resources. Apart from the council, academic departments at KNUST in Kumasi have conducted studies in agrotechnology development. Barriers to translating these inventions into process and product innovations within MSEs include two considerable obstacles. The first is the cost of scaling up far enough to use prototypes (often, inventions first come as prototypes); the cost is often considerable, and neither the research organizations nor small firms have the resources to cover it. Second, to mass-produce machines requires a good industrial base that often is not available. Most manufacturing organizations have little connection to local research, and this disconnect tends to discourage local autonomous innovation. While a number of older enterprises have built up skills in the cluster, they lack the resources needed to enter into the mass production of locally developed artifacts. Though such production is part of the mandate of Intermediate Technology Ghana, it is difficult to achieve because of resource constraints.

Several initiatives in Ghana support technology development and transfer within MSEs and encourage new ICTs. Three often-cited examples are the TCC, ITTU, and GRATIS Foundation. The TCC in Kumasi was established to act as an interface between researchers at KNUST and the business community. The ITTU was established in Suame Magazine to develop the capacity of enterprises to design, manufacture, and service equipment for agricultural and engineering development. The proliferation of small foundry businesses in other parts of Ghana can generally be credited to the Suame ITTU. The GRATIS Foundation coordinates a network of technology transfer units. The foundation has helped artisans from Suame to acquire machine tools and equipment for specialized engineering operations. Another set of policy incentives helps make ICT accessible to small firms.

Policy has also prioritized the public provision of facilities. The provision of information and communication services by private sector enterprises is conspicuous in Suame's many business and communication centers, the name commonly used in Ghana for such communal access points. Generally, these centers offer telephone calls, fax transmissions, and data-processing services at a fee. Business and communication centers can be found in both residential areas and in industrial clusters like Suame Magazine. Ghana Telecom has installed three public telephone booths within the cluster and four along the main road that fronts Suame; these are very few in the context of the cluster population.

Key Success Factors

Suame Magazine is one of the biggest clusters in Africa, with a long history of craftsmanship and entrepreneurship. It has been the object of a sustained attempt to provide public support for small business development.

The role of formal and informal associations has been important to the sustainability of the cluster. According to a survey conducted by Ghana's Department of Housing and Planning Research (DHPR 1971), as far back as the 1970s approximately 98 percent of the proprietors of Suame enterprises belonged to the Magazine Mechanical Association. Being the only umbrella association at the time, its main focus was on social functions, as noted. This was followed by an era of rapid expansion in the cluster, characterized by local economic distortions and global technological changes in the automobile industry.

In the early 1980s, the government launched a major national initiative to repair all state-owned vehicles, particularly those being used for transporting commodities such as cocoa and other food crops from the hinterland to urban areas. A new crop of young workers joined the cluster's labor force. The artisans of Suame and similar clusters were contracted to carry out the initiative using unsalvageable vehicles to repair others. This particular state policy led to the formation of the Ghana National Association of Garages, as a unified association of artisans. With its permanent national secretariat in the Suame cluster in Kumasi, the association later opened offices in Accra and other regional capitals to pursue its aims.

The aspirations and needs of motor vehicle repairers have dominated the activities of both the Ghana National Association of Garages and the Magazine Mechanical Association in almost all clusters. By contrast, little has been done for manufacturing enterprises, or for enterprises that have upgraded their activities to manufacturing. To refocus the direction of metalwork manufacturers in the cluster, the clients of the Suame ITTU came together in the late 1990s to form the Association of Micro and Small Metal industries, with the aim of addressing the constraints and challenges faced by metalwork manufacturers.

Currently, the challenges posed by globalization, local economic hardship, and growing political awareness have diminished the effectiveness of the Ghana National Association of Garages and the Magazine Mechanical Association. It appears that the majority of enterprises favor regrouping into trades—foundrymen, sprayers, auto electricians, engine reborers, and so on—to promote their enterprises. This is a departure from previous cluster networks.

Lessons Learned and Policy Implications

Qualitative and quantitative analyses (Adeya 2001) of data collected during the 1990s by the Maastricht Economic and Social Research and Training Centre on Innovation and Technology of the United Nations University (UNU-MERIT, known until January 2006 as UNU-INTECH) show that certain factors are important driving forces behind cluster performance, especially in the face of increased competition in both domestic and global markets. Firm-specific factors include: the knowledge and educational background of managing directors, increasing sales, higher profit margins, and the inclination of managers to upgrade workers' skills. Cluster-specific factors include the availability of skill-upgrading facilities within the cluster, the existence of institutions that provide technological support, and the proximity of formal training institutions.

The findings of the study suggest that a number of policy measures need to be taken by governments of developing countries to improve the competitiveness of MSE clusters. State policy should encourage greater private sector participation in setting up training and information service centers within clusters. For example, private institutions could provide need-based training. It is also recommended that managers of MSEs support process and product upgrading and, even more importantly, raise the skill level of their workforce. Organizing programs to raise managers' awareness of new machines and technologies would be one way to accomplish this. There is a need to subsidize the cost of new equipment so that new technologies become economically viable for small firms. The services of organizations specializing in business and technology development should be used to assist enterprises in adopting new technologies and generating innovations. For example, the provision of basic services such as e-mail and Internet access could make the difference between survival and demise for a small firm. Service providers could also provide small firms with information, a commodity that is often in short supply. Such initiatives, when undertaken at the cluster level, could be expected to result in better cluster performance.

One of the key recommendations the study makes is to reorganize the associations that operate in the cluster, particularly under larger umbrellas, and give them more responsibility. There is also a need for the local government to resolve the issue of land tenure to enable permanent structures to be developed in the cluster. An adequate provision of physical infrastructure is important for MSE development. With a well-organized umbrella association, some of these issues could be taken up by associations on behalf of their members.

References

Adeya, N. 2001. "The Impact and Potential of ICTs in SMMEs: A Study of Clusters in Kenya and Ghana." Maastricht: UNU/INTECH.

Dawson, J. 1988. "Small Scale Industry in Ghana: A Case of Kumasi." Report presented to ESCOR-ODA, London.

DHPR (Department of Housing and Planning Research). 1971. "Social and Economic Survey of Suame Magazine." University of Science and Technology, Kumasi, Ghana.

Ghana Statistical Service. 2002. "Population and Housing Census 2000." Accra, Ghana.

Grieco, M., N. Apt, and J. Turner, eds. 1996. *At Christmas and on Rainy Days: Transport, Travel and the Female Traders of Accra.* Aldershot: Avebury.

King, S. R. 1999. "The Role of Urban Market Women in Local Development Processes and Its Implication for Policy: A Case of Kumasi Central Market, Ghana." Ph.D. thesis submitted to the University of Sussex, UK.

McCormick, D. 1998. "Enterprise Clusters in Africa: On the Way to Industrialization?" IDS Discussion Paper 366, Nairobi, Kenya.

Obeng, G. Y. 2002. "Kumasi Suame Magazine: A Background Paper." UNU/INTECH-KITE Research Project. Kumasi, Ghana.

Velenchik, Ann D. 1995. "Apprenticeship Contracts, Small Enterprises and Credit Markets in Ghana." *World Bank Economic Review* 9(3): 451–475.

3

The Kamukunji Metalwork Cluster in Kenya

Njeri Kinyanjui

Found throughout sprawling Nairobi, small and microenterprises operating in open spaces with poor infrastructure and substandard architectural designs constitute the informal *jua kali* economy. *Jua kali*, which denotes a hot or fierce sun in Swahili, is the Kenyan name for the informal sector, where people work metal and wood in small workshops, either under the hot sun or, more recently, under crude shelters or sheds. Approximately 8 million people in Kenya are directly or indirectly employed in that economy, which accounts for about 18 percent of Kenya's GDP.[1] Commercial activities include metal, garment, and woodwork trade and manufacture; vehicle repair; and the provision of general services. These sectors are well integrated, with businesses characterized by strong back-and-forth links.

A notable feature of the *jua kali* economy is its spatial arrangement in clusters. Some have emerged spontaneously; others took shape as entrepreneurs were forced to locate in particular areas of Nairobi by city authorities. Firms are usually located in close proximity to each other in small sheds two meters square (Kinyanjui 1998). It is also common to find premises sublet to other entrepreneurs. The colocation of small and microenterprises in the cluster facilitates transactions among entrepreneurs, brokers, traders, and input suppliers.

The economic and noneconomic relationships and transactions that occur in *jua kali* clusters include flows of knowledge and technology driven by entrepreneurs' personal initiatives and client needs. Entrepreneurs learn from each other every day, whether through a simple exchange of ideas on raw materials, production, and marketing, or the full-scale copying of new product designs. On-the-job learning is common and facilitates the intergenerational transmission of knowledge and technology (Kinyanjui 2000).

Our analysis focuses on the state of knowledge and technology in the Kamukunji *jua kali* cluster—one of the oldest in Nairobi, having evolved from a spontaneous settlement of a few metal workers. The analysis is based on 20 case studies of cluster entrepreneurs, supplemented by information from officials of the Kenya National Federation of Jua Kali Associations and the Kamukunji Jua Kali Association.

Studies of cluster production strategies in Africa, especially those focused on knowledge and technology, are fairly limited. It is said that most of the clusters in

---

1. Communication from the chief executive officer of the Kenya National Federation of *Jua Kali* Associations.

Kenya, as in Africa more generally, lack dynamism and are likely to remain static unless public policy interventions are carried out (McCormick and Kinyanjui 2004; McCormick 1999). Often the conclusion drawn is that most *jua kali* clusters are at very low levels of development and need upgrading.

Several key factors prompted the decision to study the Kamukunji *jua kali* enterprise cluster. Earlier studies (McCormick 1998, 1999; Kinyanjui 1998; King 1996) describe the important role that clusters play in employment generation and wealth creation for a large number of Kenyans. These studies also highlight the specific problems that Kamukunji and other *jua kali* clusters face in their evolution as social, economic, and political entities.

Cluster Origins

The Kamukunji *jua kali* enterprise cluster occupies about 10 hectares to the east of Nairobi's central district in the so-called Eastlands. It has a population of 5,000 artisans.[2] Kenya's colonial government designated the area as a business center for native Africans, so it evolved under the colonial urban policy that segregated space on the basis of race. Business activities carried out in the cluster were restricted to small and micro enterprises that catered to African consumption patterns. Trade licenses were issued to businesses engaged in the sale of indigenous foodstuffs, repairs, and artisan manufacturing that included the production of cooking pans and hand tools to meet local household demands. During this period, the cluster served as the economic center for burgeoning settlements such as Majengo, Muthurwa, Burma, and Shauri Moyo. It also served the needs of customers and traders from rural areas, as it lay near the Machakos bus station, the terminus of buses arriving in Nairobi from the countryside. This is a location advantage that the cluster still enjoys today.

At the time of independence in 1963, most local African businesses were located in the Eastlands, and little was done to change the status quo. The Africanization strategies documented in Sessional Paper No. 10 of 1965 (Government of Kenya 1965) and subsequent five-year development plans were concerned with the Africanization of European and Asian businesses and did not address issues related to African *jua kali* businesses such as those in Kamukunji.

In postindependence Kenya, income and education levels are the most important locational determinants for businesses in the city and in the *jua kali* enterprise clusters. Most new investors in the cluster have used family and friendship networks, often of rural origin, to start businesses in the Kamukunji cluster. The cluster has served as an important access point for rural immigrants with low levels of education. Their number has significantly increased since the abolition of city migration rules and regulations.

In the first two decades following independence, governmental support of the cluster was largely absent. Like most informal settlements, the Kamukunji *jua kali* cluster was periodically subjected to efforts by city authorities to control its expansion. Authorities used the provisions of a health act to demolish buildings that were put up by entrepreneurs on the site.[3]

---

2. Communication from Kamukunji *jua kali* officials.
3. Communication from study respondent.

Academics, planners, and politicians during this period thought that modernization, industrialization, and import substitution would replace indigenous modes of production and business organization. Policy provided support to medium- and large-scale firms rather than *jua kali* businesses. As reflected in its Sessional Paper No. 10, the government changed its attitude toward *jua kali* enterprises in 1986 (Government of Kenya 1986). Since then, the cluster has received limited support from the government, donor organizations, and international financiers.[4] Recognizing the importance of Kamukunji *jua kali* enterprises in the urban and national economy, the government facilitated the construction of sheds for entrepreneurs, who until then had worked under the hot sun. The government also advised them to form *jua kali* associations to articulate the interests of entrepreneurs and facilitate future links between the government and *jua kali* businesses.

Growth Strategies

Because of its long exclusion from official policies, the *jua kali* economy in Kenya in general, and Kamukunji in particular, has had to devise strategies to survive and grow.

A survey respondent observed that knowledge and technology transfer in the cluster, essential to its growth, involves on-the-job training programs in which established artisans train young immigrants for a fee. The respondent stated that since joining the cluster in 2001, she has trained approximately 100 workers in how to make sewing machine stands. She observed that the demand for training is high and that sometimes she has been forced to turn away trainees, unable to meet the demand because of insufficient resources.

Another growth strategy involves the use of social networks. A manufacturer of potato chip cutters observed that he always turns to acquaintances who are making the same items when he needs help in joining or folding metal, or at times when a customer brings in a new product that is difficult to copy. In the cluster, there is widespread replication and imitation of imported goods or of those made locally by medium and large enterprises. This phenomenon is reflected in the making of electric chicken brooders and chaff cutters. Such knowledge and technology transfer strategies constitute the foundation of a dynamic sector that contributes significantly to employment and the production of goods and services. According to one official of the Kamukunji Jua Kali Association, 75 percent of metal boxes and 80 percent of wheelbarrows in the country are made in the cluster. This has been achieved through collective learning experiences.

The geographic location of the cluster makes it suitable for business. Its proximity to the Machakos bus station ensures that the cluster is well connected with all parts of Kenya. Its location within walking distance of both Kirinyaga Road, in the central business district, and the industrial area facilitates the movement of goods and services as well as the flow of information. The cluster's location also facilitates personal experiences and connections, such as the face-to-face meetings that are crucial to the flow of knowledge into the cluster. A Kamukunji *jua kali* entrepreneur need only walk down Kirinyaga Road to see the latest designs in metal products and machines.

---

4. Communication with *jua kali* officials.

Cluster Composition

The Kamukunji *jua kali* cluster has several metalwork subsectors. The first consists of business support services, which include scrap metal dealers, metal cutters and folders, gas and electrical welders, welding rod suppliers, and polish and paint traders. The second is composed of metal engineering producers who make folding and pressing machines and other metal-handling accessories for use within the cluster or elsewhere. Metal product manufacturers constitute the cluster's most important subsector. They are classified by the products they make. Wheelbarrows, sewing machine stands, chaff cutters, boxes, and aluminum cooking pans are some of the most important products. Others include energy-saving stoves, potato chip cutters and warmers, and equipment for use in agriculture, transport, and construction.

Worker Characteristics

One respondent observed that the cluster serves as a springboard for new entrepreneurs, not only in the cluster but in other parts of the country as well. Entry into the cluster depends on personal contacts. Once in the cluster, entrepreneurs learn how to become *jua kali* entrepreneurs and members of the *jua kali* learning society.

The fraternity of *jua kali* learning imbues individuals with the values of self-development, self-initiative, hard work, and cooperation among even competing entrepreneurs. It is because of these values that low levels of education do not deter entrepreneurs from being creative. In addition, entrepreneurs conform to the practice of doing business through interdependencies, a benefit of clustering that lone *jua kali* enterprises do not share.

The cluster contains a mix of individuals with varying education levels. Out of the 20 case study respondents, 7 had completed secondary school, while 6 had only primary education. Five of the respondents were Kenya Polytechnic graduates, and two were university graduates. In terms of skill level, only five had skill certificates from the Directorate of Industrial Training. The rest obtained skills on the job and had not had their skill level certified. Most of the respondents (17) obtained skills from friends, while 3 obtained their skills from relatives. This information further reinforces the role of social networks in knowledge and technology transfer.

Firm Characteristics

The cluster is dominated by small enterprises (4–10 workers) and microenterprises (1–3 workers) that are located close to each other; some even share the same shed. A shed can house as many as three different entrepreneurs. Among the enterprises studied three had 10 workers, seven had 5 workers, and ten had no employees other than the owner. Trainees are an important feature in the cluster. Training is mainly practical and is the main medium of knowledge and skill transfer. Some trainers have as many as five trainees ages 15–20 years.

Customers and Markets

The cluster serves local, national, and regional markets (mainly Uganda and Rwanda). Nairobi and its environs make up the largest source of customers. Wheelbarrows, sewing machine stands, and boxes are the main products distributed in the national and regional markets. Chicken troughs and chaff cutters are sold to customers in rural areas. Potato chip cutters, deep fryers, and warmers are sold in small towns as well as in the city of Nairobi. Most enterprises have regular customers; some originate from entrepreneurs' rural villages, while others belong to the same ethnic group.

Knowledge and Technology in the Kamukunji *Jua Kali* Cluster

To succeed, firms require immense knowledge to facilitate their decision-making processes in production, the sourcing of raw materials, and customer relationships. The search for knowledge in *jua kali* businesses is a continuous process that is not deterred by entrepreneurs' low levels of education, limited investment capacity, and limited research and development. According to one respondent, in-cluster competition between artisans is a major factor contributing to skill development and subsequent technological advancement. Another respondent observed that the collective knowledge within the cluster helps individual entrepreneurs be innovative, giving the entire cluster a competitive edge over others in the city and the rest of the country.

Types

Firms in the Kamukunji *jua kali* cluster mainly use manual technologies in their production processes. New technology is often beyond workers' levels of education and skills. Entrepreneurs collaborate and are flexible enough to adapt to changes in manual technologies in the cluster.

According to four entrepreneurs in the case study, most cluster entrepreneurs have a thorough understanding of metal qualities and accessories. In production, they are conversant with engineering processes and the skills of bending, folding, pressing, and joining metals to make items such as telephone booths, aluminum cooking pots, chaff cutters, and chip warmers. They also exhibit knowledge in production design.

As a marketing strategy, entrepreneurs exploit their colocation with other businesses. They also use on-site brokers who direct customers to specific producers. These brokers are paid a commission on every product purchased by a customer. The more aggressive entrepreneurs hawk their products to hardware shops and retailers in the city center. In addition, entrepreneurs take advantage of annual *jua kali* exhibitions organized by the Ministry of Labor and the Kenya National Federation of Jua Kali Associations (KNFJA) in Nairobi, Kampala, and Dar-es-Salaam.

Sources

Knowledge and technology are often acquired through informal learning in the cluster. For the *jua kali* entrepreneur, the road to accumulating and generating knowledge and technology is still rough despite the advantages of being in a cluster. Self-initiative, creativity, risk-taking, endurance, and drive are attributes that *jua kali* entrepreneurs throughout Kenya, including those in Kamukunji, must have. The cost of seeking knowledge and technology through self-initiative, trial and error, frequent frustrations, and expenditures of time and money is relatively high compared to larger firms or formal sectors, which often have access to formal or nonformal learning.

Instead of *jua kali* technicians being hostile competitors, however, they generally share mutual trust. This trust facilitates technological spillover and learning processes. Almost all entrepreneurs have someone who helped them, or whom they helped, in joining the cluster. These acquaintances are relatives and friends, and often come from the same rural origins.

Entrepreneurs' self-initiatives are enhanced by peer-learning networks in the cluster. Together, peers design and make products similar to those manufactured in formal enterprises, whether imported or simply brought in by customers. These peer networks evolve after long periods of association and facilitate informal joint action. The networks define the rules and regulations of learning, and are both real and virtual. Used when the need arises, they develop through personal connections, fraternity, ethnicity, sector groups, and associations.

Customers—including individuals, households, and traders—are a vital source of cluster knowledge and technology. Customers bring product designs to *jua kali* entrepreneurs, who use their own intuition and know-how to create custom-made products.

Recognized and well-established *jua kali* trainers are also sources of knowledge and technology. Most are technicians who have accumulated technical knowledge in metalwork and are able to imitate designs of new products on the market. Some respondents said they have up to 14 years of training in the cluster. On-the-job training takes place through observation and practical activities.

Technology Transfer

The transfer of knowledge and technology between non-*jua kali* firms and the Kamukunji *jua kali* cluster is indirect. It takes place through former factory workers who, after being laid off, seek self-employment in the cluster. They use the knowledge gained in previous employment to make products similar to the ones they had made in factories. Other sources of knowledge and technology transfer are workers from large companies who come to work in the cluster during their free time, especially during weekends, or run businesses parallel to their jobs. These entrepreneurs transfer skills to the cluster and become members of virtual joint-action networks. The entrepreneurs imitate and copy products from local industries. This is reflected in the making of telephone stands copied from those used in the post office.

Apart from a few graduates of polytechnics and local universities who have businesses in the cluster, there is little evidence that these institutions influence technology and knowledge dynamism. None of the graduates in the case studies reported to have links with their previous institutions. Moreover, these graduates are too few to compose a critical mass that would affect technology and knowledge development in the cluster.

State Policies

The formation of the Kamukunji Jua Kali Welfare Organization was a government initiative. A membership organization linked to the KNFJA, it was created to encourage vertical joint action among *jua kali* entrepreneurs in initiatives such as buying land. The organization was also established to serve as the avenue through which the government would communicate policies and interventions to *jua kali* entrepreneurs.

Some of the joint actions carried out by the Kamukunji Jua Kali Welfare Association, in conjunction with the Ministry of Human Resources and Labor, include trade exhibitions and skill development programs. Intervention projects sponsored by UN organizations and international financial organizations have also been channeled through *jua kali* associations. Examples are the Voucher Training Program for Skill Development, the establishment of the Ziwani Learning and Demonstration Center, and the Kariobangi Training Center.

Explicit policies promoting knowledge and skills in *jua kali* enterprises gained ground in the 1980s. The government's changed attitude toward *jua kali* workers at the time was spurred by social and political crises in the country. The effects of structural adjustment policies and slipping support for the government among the formal sector elite prompted the government to look more favorably on *jua kali* economic initiatives. The Kamukunji *jua kali* cluster was among the first beneficiaries of government projects geared toward the sector.

A national campaign promoting environmental conservation brings knowledge and technology to the clusters. For example, some entrepreneurs quickly copied energy-saving cooking stoves developed by KENGO, a local nongovernmental organization. The stoves' high market demand induced other entrepreneurs to adopt and modify the same technology. Other efforts to support the sector include the creation of the Department of Micro and Small Enterprises Development in the Ministry of Labor. Because of political questions of marginalization, social exclusion, and the volatile nature of poverty and ethnicity, policies meant for the *jua kali* sector are received by the intended beneficiaries with some skepticism. Entrepreneurs are suspicious of state policies, and typically only a few respond to them. It is no wonder, then, that most of the entrepreneurs interviewed in the 20 case studies felt that both local and national governments do not support *jua kali* entrepreneurs, especially in knowledge and technology issues. Also, most of the entrepreneurs interviewed do not pay membership fees or attend meetings when they are called.

Incentives

The Sessional Paper No. 2 of 2005 on the Development of Micro and Small Enterprises for Wealth and Employment Creation recognized the limited access to skills and technology experienced by micro and small enterprises (MSEs).

> Kenya's MSEs are characterized by restricted levels of technology, inappropriate technology, and inadequate institutional capacity to support adaptation and absorption of modern technological skills. In addition, they also suffer lack of information on existing technologies and their potential for increased trade. Specifically, MSEs suffer a weak environment that hampers coordination and transfer of appropriate technology. Consequently, the sector continues to experience low productivity, poor quality and limited range of products resulting in low competitiveness of the MSE products (Government of Kenya 2005: 12).

In response to the technological demands of MSEs, the government proposed the following:

- A policy framework that seeks to enhance the ability of MSEs to adopt and adapt new technology. This would be done by improving institutions that support technology development, thereby increasing overall access to information and technical skills. Five major institutions—the Kenya Industrial Research Development Institute, National Council of Science and Technology, Kenya Industrial Estates, Kenya Bureau of Standards, and the Productivity Center of Kenya—were charged with reviewing the current modes of technology acquisition and transfer. First, they were to come up with laws and legislation that would regulate and promote local and international technology transfer. Second, they were to encourage subcontracting, franchising, and licensing partnerships. Finally, they were to be involved in the vetting and registration of imported technologies.

- Recognizing that the local capacity to create technology is low and that technology therefore must be imported from China, India, Republic of Korea, Pakistan, and elsewhere, the government planned to waive the duty on basic engineering machinery. For this to be done, MSE-specific needs were to be identified and suggestions for appropriate technologies given to the Department of Micro and Small Enterprises Development in the Ministry of Labor. Efforts to encourage the commercialization of technology and to enhance research and development were other priorities the government sought to address. Those were to be realized by strengthening links between MSEs and universities, technical institutions, and research bodies.
- An MSE development technology fund was to be initiated to finance research and development. Other initiatives to be undertaken within the policy framework were to improve access to the existing intellectual property system, promote skill acquisition and development, and reorganize MSE primary associations along sectoral lines.

The sessional paper does not offer any specific incentives for promoting MSEs beyond calling for the waiver of import duties on basic engineering machinery. The policy also is not cluster-specific. It is too general and does not demonstrate how collective efficiency, knowledge, and technology flows would be diversified and advanced to enhance growth in the cluster.

Although well intended, the policy appears to be a top-down approach to technology transfer, whereby MSE entrepreneurs will be the recipients of what is produced by universities, technical institutions, and research bodies. No initiative has focused on planning interventions from sources known to be well received among cluster entrepreneurs.

The creativity of entrepreneurs in combining production factors to come up with products also has not been integrated in strategies based on cluster experience. This is unfortunate, because it is quite possible that, by working together with universities and government institutions, MSEs could generate formidable knowledge and technology growth.

Key Success Factors

Cluster-specific success factors include technological innovation, knowledge, skills, market access, and organizational production (table 3.1).

Kamukunji *jua kali* entrepreneurs often observe new products in the market, study them, and design methods of producing similar products or others that can serve the same purpose. The evolution of skills, energized by the flow of informa-

Table 3.1. *Key success factors*

Factors	Cluster-specific	National
Innovation; new methods of production, utilization of raw materials, and design	*	
Skill development and knowledge (growth and flow of new knowledge in the cluster)	*	
Quality and durability of products	*	
Business management	*	
Product technology	*	
Geographic location		*
Availability of markets	*	*
Production of multiple products	*	

Source: Author's information.

tion in the cluster, facilitates success in other clusters nationally. The Kamukunji cluster's unique specialization in metalwork also makes it stand out from other clusters in the country. Firm organization, translated into good management practices, enhances the flow of information vital to both production and marketing.

Levels of product diversification provide a clear advantage in terms of interdependence and subcontracting among firms. They also allow the customer to find everything he or she needs under one collection of roofs. Geographic proximity to the main bus terminus allows rural customers coming for metal agricultural products to easily access the cluster. This also applies to traders who buy products from the cluster for sale in other parts of the country. The cluster's proximity to the industrial area and Kirinyaga Road ensures the availability of raw materials.

The cluster is able to build on its past experience. It has survived three major technological generations. At each stage, it has been able to adapt and change machinery used in the past to make new products. The cluster learns from past mistakes to survive and grow.

Knowledge is a key success factor in the cluster. Study respondents observed that the cluster has its own unique knowledge base. Information flows between entrepreneurs, who learn from each other quickly. Innovators allow others to copy and adapt new technology. This flow of knowledge has enhanced the survival of the cluster. A metal box maker, for example, will paint his box blue; another one will add white dots or bind the sharp edges of the box. This way of doing things is quickly adopted by other metal box makers in the cluster, with each adding a new feature. One of the respondents said that this kind of knowledge improvement was the chief reason for the cluster's success.

The cluster's knowledge and technology base has evolved with limited influence from national polytechnics, universities, and other technical institutes. The 20 respondents did not view fresh graduates from national institutes of technology, national polytechnics, or universities as sources of knowledge in the cluster. This is one area that needs further investigation because the government is planning a link between the *jua kali* sector and local institutions of knowledge transfer (institutes of technology, technical institutes, and universities). It is not clear which niche of cluster knowledge these institutions would support.

Lessons Learned and Policy Implications

Knowledge and technology in the Kamukunji *jua kali* enterprise cluster are dynamic, evolving, and abundant, though at a low level. They form the basis for the survival and growth of businesses. The cluster's main sources of knowledge are the entrepreneurs themselves, and a web of social relations conveys knowledge and technological spillovers among enterprises. To date the attempts of state and donor agencies to intervene in the cluster's technology and knowledge transfer have yielded limited success.

Human capital development is realized through on-the-job training of younger entrepreneurs. Most of the skills and technology in the cluster are obtained through personal relationships and face-to-face interaction. The cluster attracts entrepreneurs with low levels of education, most with only a primary or secondary school education. Once an entrepreneur joins the cluster, he or she undergoes a process of adaptation that involves skill drills and hard work.

Entrepreneurs have limited relationships with local technical institutes, youth polytechnics, national polytechnics, and universities. A combination of indigenous artisanal skills and standard technological processes is found in the cluster. As noted, most skills are acquired on the job either through training or by dismantling and reassembling products.

Challenges Facing the Cluster

Policy and political will. There appears to be a mismatch between policy and the political will to implement it. All the entrepreneurs interviewed for this study felt that the government had neglected them. They said that though they had heard of funding and training programs for the *jua kali,* these programs did not reach them.

No mechanism facilitates the movement of information and knowledge from the government bureaucracy to the cluster. The local authorities responsible for the Kamukunji *jua kali* cluster appear to be chiefly concerned with the collection of rate payments and trade licenses. According to one respondent, in his 15 years at the Kamukunji cluster, he has never seen any improvement of sanitation facilities or streets to facilitate movement. He also said that the rate at which local authorities collect money from him does not match the rate of improvement in the provision of services.

Heavy turnover of employees and trainees. There is a substantial movement of employees and trainees in the cluster. Trainees and employees move out to start their own businesses after gaining experience and raising money in or outside the cluster. Labor contracts are largely informal and not binding. Most workers are paid by project and can quit whenever they wish, without giving notice.

Lack of certification from on-the-job training. Trainers have not recognized the importance of issuing training certificates to employees. One respondent asserted that his profession did not require the possession of certificates. He also said that employees are there to gain skills that enable them to earn a living through self-employment, and that certificates are for those in schools. The issue of providing certificates does not seem to have been raised by cluster associations or the ministry concerned.

Lack of links between the cluster and learning institutions. Although students from learning institutions such as the polytechnics in Nairobi, Mombasa, and Eldoret intern and train at the Kamukunji enterprise cluster, there is not yet any formal link between the cluster and such institutions. Some respondents claimed that graduates from these institutions lack practical experience.

Poor infrastructure, overcrowding, and substandard architectural designs. Sheds and other structures in the Kamukunji cluster were constructed in the 1980s and meant for only a few artisans. The population has since increased to 5,000. With overcrowding, it is difficult for entrepreneurs to guard their trade secrets since all production work is done in the open. Questions arise about when technological and knowledge spillover are positive for growth and when they involve the illegal imitation of other people's work.

Recommendations

Sanitation, lighting and electricity for industrial use, and links between the cluster and learning institutions—all must be upgraded if the cluster is to continue to grow and become more productive. There is also a need to make the *jua kali* associations more responsive to the needs of entrepreneurs. This can be done through regular elections and by writing all-inclusive association constitutions that recognize local institutions and organizations based on the clusters' social and cultural interactions. Second, each association should be directed toward business concerns, becoming more of an advocacy organization and professional association. *Jua kali* associations could be better linked with other business associations and local chambers of commerce.

Knowledge and technological spillover and transfer could be enhanced if the image and visibility of the cluster were improved. Local learning institutions could play a critical role if they viewed *jua kali* enterprises through the *jua kali* lens. This would involve the appreciation of the cluster's ability to evolve its own organizations based on relationships, as well as the acknowledgement of local, self-initiated knowledge and technology transfer.

There is also a need to integrate the learning processes found in the Kamukunji *jua kali* cluster with those in learning institutions so that students can be exposed to both theoretical and practical knowledge. Entrepreneurs need both practical and theoretical knowledge. They need to know government polices and marketing tactics. Support organizations should recognize already existing learning institutions. Efforts should be geared toward expanding peer-learning networks into continuous lifelong learning institutions for generating knowledge and technology in the cluster.

References

Government of Kenya. 1965. "African Socialism and Its Application to Development." Sessional Paper 10. Nairobi: Government Printer.

———. 1986. "Economic Management for Renewed Growth." Sessional Paper 1. Nairobi: Government Printer.

———. 2005. "Development of Micro and Small Enterprises for Wealth and Employment Creation for Poverty Reduction." Sessional Paper 2. Nairobi: Government Printer.

King, K. 1996. *Jua Kali Kenya: Change and Development in an Informal Economy 1970–1995.* Nairobi: East African Educational Publishers.

Kinyanjui, M. N. 1998. "Ziwani and Kigandani Jua Kali Enterprise Clusters: Do Small Businesses Gain by Being in Close Proximity to Each Other." *Journal of African Research and Development* 27/28: 270–290.

————. 2000. "Tapping Opportunities in Jua Kali Enterprise Clusters: The Case of Ziwani and Kigandaini." IDS Working Paper 525. Institute for Development Studies, University of Nairobi.

McCormick, D. 1998. "Enterprise Clusters in Africa: From Collective Efficiency to Industrialisation." Report prepared as part of a research project on collective efficiency and small enterprises in Kenya. Institute for Development Studies, University of Nairobi.

————. 1999. "African Enterprise Clusters and Industrialization: Theory and Reality." *World Development* 27(9): 1531–1551.

McCormick, D., and M. N. Kinyanjui. 2004. "Industrializing Kenya: Building Capacity of Micro and Small Enterprises." September Working Paper 15, University of Leipzig.

4

The Lake Naivasha Cut Flower Cluster in Kenya

Maurice Ochieng Bolo

Kenya's cut flower industry has grown steadily in acres, volume, and value over the last 10 years (table 4.1). Industry exports increased from 29,373 tons (worth KSh 3.6 billion) in 1995 to 60,982 tons (worth KSh 16.5 billion) in 2003. The industry has been expanding at an annual rate of 200 hectares, one of the most rapid expansions reported in any country in the world.[1] The cut flower industry constitutes more than 60 percent of the country's horticultural sector, contributing about 1.5 percent[2] of the national GDP and up to 8 percent of the country's total export revenues. The Kenya Flower Council (KFC) estimates that the flower industry contributes US$200 million annually to Kenya's economy and employs nearly two million people both directly and indirectly.

Kenya's cut flower industry is the largest single source of flowers imported into the European Union (EU), providing up to 25 percent of total flower imports, ahead of Colombia (17 percent) and Israel (16 percent). Kenya exports 60,000 tons of flowers into the European Union annually, with floral varieties dominated by roses (more than 70 percent), carnations, *Hypericum*, *Alstroemeria*, and *Eryngium*. Apart from Holland, where the bulk of Kenya's flowers are exported (more than 65 percent), export destinations include the United Kingdom, Germany, France, and Switzerland (table 4.2).

The success of the cut flower industry in Kenya has been attributed to a combination of factors—among them Kenya's natural resources (particularly agro-climatic conditions), the active participation of a robust private sector, and favorable government policies (Bolo 2005). Because of its location at the equator, Kenya has ideal agro-climatic conditions for the year-round production of flowers. Temperatures range from 22–30 degrees Celsius during the day to 6–12 degrees at night. The government's involvement in the flower industry is largely limited to licensing and regulation, leaving ample room for active private sector participation in the industry. General policy provides a favorable environment, with adequate institutions to support development.

---

1. See the *East African,* May 2–8, 2005 (http://www.nationmedia.com/eastafrican/current/index.html).
2. Horticulture contributes 2.5 percent of Kenya's GDP according to Kenya's Horticultural Crops Development Authority. Floriculture constitutes 60 percent of this total.

Table 4.1. Growth in floricultural exports, 1995–2004

Year	Value (KSh billion)	Tons
1995	3.643	29,373
1996	4.366	35,212
1997	4.900	35,850
1998	5.913	30,220
1999	7.234	36,992
2000	7.270	38,756
2001	10.624	41,396
2002	14.792	52,106
2003	16.495	60,982
2004	18.719	70,666
2005	22,897	81,217

Source: HCDA.

Table 4.2. Major export destinations of Kenya's floral exports, 2003

Country	Quantity exported	Percent of total floricultural exports
Holland	40,077	65.7
United Kingdom	12,087	19.8
Germany	4,267	7.0
France	1,574	2.6
Switzerland	1,061	1.7

Source: HCDA.

Industry Profile

The Horticultural Crops Development Authority (HCDA) estimates that there are more than 160 growers of cut flowers in Kenya. These are categorized as small-scale (under 4 hectares), medium-scale (10–20 hectares), and large-scale (more than 50 hectares). There are no standard employment figures, but, according to our estimates, small-scale farms employ up to 350 workers, medium-scale farms between 500 and 1,000, and large-scale farms 1,000 to 2,000 workers.[3]

The industry is dominated by large companies, which grow up to 97 percent of total flower exports and are mostly owned by foreigners or Kenyans of foreign descent. Small-scale growers contribute a mere 3 percent to total flower exports. This imbalance is explained by the high capital- and knowledge-intensive nature of the flower business, as well as strict regulatory market requirements that have locked out most small-scale growers. According to HCDA, small-scale production has been declining over the last five years because of increased competition and

---

3. These are average estimates obtained from discussions with several farm managers. The figures fluctuate during peak and off-peak seasons.

Table 4.3. Distribution of flower farms in Kenya by major growing region, 2005

Region	Area (hectares)
Naivasha	872.5
Thika	251.7
Kiambu/Limuru	187.6
Nairobi	221.6
Nakuru	173.6
Nanyuki/Nyahururu	45.5
Mt. Kenya region	118.5
Eldoret	129.5
Total	2,000.5

Source: Compiled by author from *Floriculture Magazine* data.

Table 4.4. Distribution of the most important floral varieties grown in Kenya

Variety	Area (hectares)
Roses	812
Carnations	211
Hypericum	18.4
Alstroemeria	57.6
Eryngium	201.5

Source: HCDA.

limited access to improved varieties. It is estimated that capital investment in flower production requires approximately US$50,000 per hectare in addition to a vigorous marketing network. These requirements have confined most small-scale growers to summer flowers that can be grown outdoors and do not require heavy investment in greenhouses and sophisticated technologies.

It is estimated that more than 2,000 hectares of Kenya's agricultural land are being used to grow cut flowers,[4] with the major growing regions concentrated around Lake Naivasha, Thika, Limuru, Nairobi, and the Athi river plain. Further upcountry, significant growing areas include Nakuru, Nanyuki and Nyahururu, the Mt. Kenya region, and Eldoret (see table 4.3). The Lake Naivasha cluster accounts for about 44 percent of the total area used for cut flowers. The distribution of flower varieties is listed in table 4.4, with the greatest percentage of total area being used

---

4. This estimate is based on a recent survey conducted by *Floriculture Magazine,* the official journal of the Association of Kenya Floriculturalists. It is important to note, however, that the survey focused on export companies and farms and may not have captured the small-holders who are either outdoor growers or deal only in summer flowers and sell locally. The total hectarage used for cut flowers is probably higher than the estimate. The data are derived from ongoing work to be published in the *Floriculture Kenya Handbook 2006* by Scoop Communications, Ltd. This publication has compiled all the exporting flower farms and firms, their total hectarage (both current and planned), locations, and contacts in Kenya.

for roses. Kiptum (2005) has noted that "floriculture in Kenya is dominated by 24 large companies [that] make up over 72 percent of total flower exports and own, on average, between 20–100 hectares, employing a workforce of 250–6,000 persons." Small companies usually grow on 5 to 20 hectares and are less capital-intensive; they usually do some growing in open fields and do not export year-round. Small farms grow summer flowers including *Eryngium, Ornithogalum,* papyrus, lilies, *Ammi, Moluccella, Asclepias, Rudbeckia, Euphorbia,* orchids, and *Scabiosa.* Large-scale farms have strong marketing arms, often established as sister companies in Europe. These help sale and distribution efforts and provide market information that is used to direct operations. Small growers have difficulty accessing export markets because of the high cost of freight and strict phytosanitary requirements.

The Lake Naivasha Cluster

The Lake Naivasha region is the hub of Kenya's cut flower industry. It is situated about 100 kilometers northwest of Nairobi in the Great Rift Valley, 1,800–2,000 meters above sea level. Average regional temperatures range between 7.3 and 22.7 degrees Celsius; annual rainfall ranges from 156 millimeters to 1,134 millimeters per month, distributed throughout the year with peaks in April and May, during the long rains, and October and November, during the short rains.

It is estimated that more than 50 percent of the country's total flower production is concentrated around Lake Naivasha. Other than growers, the Lake Naivasha cluster contains other key industry actors including research institutions, breeding farms, quality control and regulatory agencies, input suppliers, credit and finance institutions, trade promotion agencies, and intermediary organizations. The emergence and growth of the Lake Naivasha cluster has been attributed to several factors, including:

- *Availability of freshwater resources for irrigation.* Lake Naivasha is the only freshwater lake in the Rift Valley region. Flower growing requires a lot of water for irrigation, and the presence of Lake Naivasha attracted farmers to the region. Besides the lake, there are underground water resources (aquifers) that the farms tap for irrigation purposes.
- *Large farms for large-scale commercial production.* The availability of large tracts of land around Lake Naivasha with soils suitable for flower production contributed to cluster development. Historically, these large tracts of land were owned (through leasehold) by white settlers. For example, Lord Delamere Estates owns most of the land around the town of Naivasha. Both white settlers and the government have leased out fallow land to large-scale commercial flower growers.
- *Soil and climate conducive to horticultural production.* The soils, temperature, and annual rainfall of Lake Naivasha provide favorable conditions for cut flower production.
- *Proximity to Jomo Kenyatta International Airport.* With its location on the Nairobi–Nakuru highway, approximately one hour from the city center, the Naivasha cluster has easy access to Nairobi's international airport. Nairobi is considered a major hub of the East African region; major airlines accord Kenya easy access into Europe and other parts of the world.

Knowledge, Technology, and Networking in the Lake Naivasha Cluster

Our analysis of the Lake Naivasha cluster focuses on how knowledge and technology are acquired and disseminated within the cluster, and how its different actors interact with and learn from each other.

Most of the key actors in the cut flower industry agree that Kenya has the human and technical competence and skills required to ensure competitiveness in the industry (Bolo 2005). This human capital base is buttressed by research, institutes for education and training such as the National Horticultural Research Center, and several universities that offer training programs in horticulture. However, the industry has not fully utilized the country's existing research capacity to solve the problems it faces. Instead, it has relied heavily on expatriates for technical advice and assistance.

Most flower farm owners (or directors) are businessmen who have acquired their knowledge through extensive experience in the flower business and have a very good understanding of the industry. Some are graduates of horticulture programs. Most have inherited their farms through family ties, and many have been in the business all their lives. In most cases, they employ horticulture graduates as farm managers to deal with the technical details of production, while the farm owners themselves serve as directors dealing with administration and product marketing.

The flower industry has long operated as a closed system, with little formal interaction between farms and other actors. This has been attributed to lack of trust between farms and the need to guard trade secrets. However, pressure from environmental and human rights groups, consumer demands to know about the working conditions of flower farm workers, and the negative publicity these have generated have obliged flower farms to gradually open up to the public. Regular (and often unannounced) environmental and social audits are conducted to ensure that farms not only conform to good agricultural practices, but also maintain environmental standards and favorable working conditions. Compliance is enforced through codes of practice and certification by industry associations such as the KFC, Fresh Produce Exporters Association of Kenya (FPEAK), Horticultural Ethical Business Initiative, Lake Naivasha Growers Group, Lake Naivasha Riparian Association, and Kenya Bureau of Standards. A horizontal flow of information is common among flower farms and occurs through a combination of informal and nonformal learning and labor mobility:

- Farms learn from their neighbors through exchange of information on market and new technologies, as well as through farm visits and excursions organized by industry organizations.
- Farms learn from each other through seminars organized by support institutions, the government, and donors.
- "Poaching" and labor mobility are common, with the most skilled workers always the most sought after. These workers often transfer their knowledge and skills to their new farms, while their continued, informal interactions with former colleagues allow them to compare notes about farm operations.
- Farm owners hire expatriates and technical experts from abroad to train employees in various techniques. Farm workers mainly learn through observation and on-the-job training.

Human Capital and the Role of Higher Education

The majority of entrepreneurs in the flower industry, especially in large-scale operations, hold a bachelor's degree (and some have postgraduate qualifications) either in horticulture or business administration and management. Most of those with a university education hold management positions, while the majority of laborers have not gone beyond secondary school training. Among small-scale growers (again, mainly locals dealing in summer flowers), the majority of entrepreneurs have a formal education up to the secondary school level and no specialized training either in horticulture or business management. This low level of education among small-scale farmers has compounded the problems they face in the industry, given that they also lack the financial resources needed to hire experts to manage their farms. In large farms, if a deficiency in particular skills or knowledge is found, expatriates can be hired from abroad to fill the gap. Most farms do not have formal training programs for their employees. When employees have been sponsored for specialized training, this has been on an ad hoc basis dictated by the urgent skill requirements of either expansion or the upgrading of farm activities. The high staff turnover that results from employee "poaching" among competitor farms is a disincentive to training. Farms fear investing heavily in training only to lose their most highly trained employees to their competitors.

Kenya's universities continue to train highly skilled manpower for the industry, and almost all public universities have programs in horticulture. Some universities have introduced floriculture as an independent course to address the specific needs of the flower sector. For example, Jomo Kenyatta University of Agriculture and Technology (www.jkuat.ac.ke) offers degree programs in ornamental science and landscaping in which third-year students take courses in production of cut flowers and cut foliage. Floriculture is also offered as an area of specialization at the master's level. Maseno University (www.maseno.ac.ke) offers floriculture both at the master's and doctoral levels, focusing on flower production in Kenya, while floriculture is offered as a unit course in horticultural degree programs.

Universities have also tried to forge closer links with the industry, and some have initiated joint programs in research and training designed especially for postgraduate students. Undergraduate horticulture students also spend time during their training as interns in Kenyan farms. However, curricula must be continuously updated to reflect industry needs as well as to train more technical staff, at diploma levels, to work with farmers.

Technology Spillover and Transfer

As markets become more competitive, using outdated technology can easily push a company out of business. Because of this, farms tend to keep track of the latest technological developments in flower production. The flower industry has continued to adapt to the changing technological environment, as can be seen in the phasing out of outdoor growing and the replacement of wooden greenhouses with the latest technologies in steel greenhouses. There also has been a shift to hydroponics to grow some varieties such as carnations. Surface irrigation has been replaced by drip irrigation over the years, and now "fertigation" techniques are being used. Clustering and the interactions it fosters influence industry methods, materials, markets, and the varieties grown. Other important factors in the choice of technologies include cost, reliability and availability of technical support, and the farmer's previous experience. Marketing companies and distributors of farm input supplies also influence technology choices. Since farms are clustered in one geographic area, it is not unusual to find several farms using similar technologies, their decisions having been influenced by the same marketing companies.

Market Access and Technical Assistance

Outsourcing and subcontracting schemes are commonly found between large and small farms. These are often driven by the need of smaller farms to penetrate export markets, while allowing them to avoid the high industry costs associated with freight and marketing. Small farms that fail to get the accreditation or certification they need to sell directly in export markets can sell through large farms that act as middlemen. Subcontracting also becomes necessary when large farms are unable to grow certain varieties in demand either because of unfavorable climatic conditions or because the demand is short-term and does not justify investment in extra operational costs.

In short, large farms subcontract with smaller farms to grow and supply flowers. Large farms market on behalf of small farms and, in return, provide pre- and postharvest advice and technical expertise to ensure that flower supplies meet market standards. In addition to the contractual arrangements made between small and large farms, there are companies that specialize in exporting flowers but do not produce their own. Such companies contract farmers to grow certain varieties of flowers depending on prevailing market demands. In return, the companies offer agronomic advice, source seeds and other inputs, and provide informal training. Usually such companies employ technical experts who visit farmers on a regular basis during the growing periods to ensure a good-quality supply. These subcontracting arrangements are usually cemented by detailed contracts.

Collaboration and Joint Action

The Lake Naivasha cluster demonstrates examples of cooperation and collaboration arising from the deliberate, conscious efforts of different actors. Flower farms have formed various industrial associations with various objectives—among them lobbying for policy support, maintaining environmental conservation and product quality standards, and facilitating corporate social responsibility programs. The KFC and FPEAK are the key industry associations for maintaining standards, facilitating market access, and gathering market intelligence for their members. These associations have increased the bargaining power of growers in matters of freight charges, taxation, and input prices, and have even won against unfavorable policies. The Horticultural Ethical Business Initiative conducts regular social audits to ensure that workers' welfare is maintained. In all these cases, members are graded on their level of performance and adherence to the codes of practice agreed on by the various associations.

In the field of environmental conservation and the sustainable use of the natural resources around Lake Naivasha, two key associations stand out: the Lake Naivasha Growers Group and the Lake Naivasha Riparian Association. The first was formed in the late 1990s in response to complaints that horticultural farms around the lake were not environmentally and socially responsible. The association's membership embraces all stakeholders involved in intensive agricultural activities around Lake Naivasha. Members benefit from regular environmental and social auditing, training, and relevant information. The diverse membership of the Lake Naivasha Riparian Association includes small holders, ranchers, flower growers, tour operators, the Kenya Wildlife Service, the Kenya Power and Lighting Company, and the Naivasha municipal council. The association has developed a comprehensive management plan to control human activities in the area and protect the lake from depletion.

There also has been an increase in the provision of local community amenities such as health services and schools. These are provided by farms as part of their social responsibility programs. Flower farms around Lake Naivasha have come together to support these social programs and to pool their resources for infrastructure development. For example, flower farms have invested up to KSh 25 million in the repair and construction of parts of the Moi South Lake Road, which serves most of the farms around the lake.

Foreign Cooperation in the Flower Industry

There is a strong connection between Kenya's flower industry and international companies and organizations. The links include collaborations in training, laboratory analysis and diagnosis, technology acquisition, and marketing.

TRAINING AND CAPACITY BUILDING Most foreign-supported training and capacity building in the industry are geared toward achieving and maintaining high-quality standards for export products.

- The Royal Netherlands Embassy in Nairobi initiated a training program to improve local horticultural producers' access to markets in industrial countries.[5] The program targets mid-level managers and small farmers. The program has begun with vocational training for sector managers, conducted by registered local NGOs whose representatives receive basic training from the embassy. When skills are not available in-country, the embassy helps find international sources.
- The Flower Labor Program of Germany has collaborated with the International Center for Insect Physiology and Ecology in Kenya to develop program to train "flower scouts." Targeting supervisors and management staff in the production units of flower farms, the program enables new scouts to detect problems and diseases early enough to avoid extensive crop damage.
- Following complaints about working conditions on flower farms, the Ethical Trading Initiative funded a training program for the flower industry in 2003. This emphasized the role of participatory social auditing to ensure that human and environmental health requirements are met. The training raised industry awareness and resulted in the formation of the Horticultural Ethical Business Initiative, is a Kenyan version of the Ethical Trading Initiative centered in Britain.

---

5. For more on this program, see *Floriculture Magazine*, March/April 2006.

LABORATORY ANALYSIS AND DIAGNOSIS The Kenyan flower industry works very closely with laboratories and research institutes in developed countries. This is partly motivated by the fact that consumers tend to trust the analysis and tests conducted by these laboratories more, so their approval boosts farms' export sales. In addition, these laboratories are less bureaucratic and provide timely responses to farmers, sometimes via e-mail within three days. Participants in such collaborations include the Société Générale de Surveillance, Relab de Haan Laboratories, Bureau Veritas, and Milieu Programa Sieerteelt.

TECHNOLOGY ACQUISITION Most flower industry technologies are sourced from abroad, requiring cooperation between Kenyan farms and the foreign companies supplying the technologies. For example, most greenhouses are imported from Israel and Spain, both of which have company representatives stationed in Kenya. Also, stocks for most exported flower varieties are imported; their breeding companies have local representatives and branches in Kenya involved in propagation and distribution.

RESEARCH Several collaborative research programs join Kenyan companies and farms with research institutes based in developed countries. An example is the program of Dudutech (K) Ltd., an integrated pest management company based in Kenya that provides crop-protection solutions to the Kenyan horticultural industry. Its parent company, Flamingo Holdings, in collaboration with sister companies in the United Kingdom (such as Flamingo U.K. Ltd and Flower Plus—both leading suppliers of fresh produce and flowers to supermarkets and retailers), has been involved in research in integrated pest management and was recently awarded the prestigious Environmental Award for Crop Protection for its achievements in Kenya. Dudutech is now mass-producing a range of pest fighters including amblyseius, phytoseiulus, encarsia, and aphidius.

Policies and Incentives

A favorable policy environment has been instrumental in the success of the cut flower industry in Kenya. The government of Kenya recognized the important role of horticulture in the national economy as early as 1966 and committed itself to promoting industry growth. This commitment was first demonstrated in 1967, when horticulture was declared a special crop and accorded priority in the government's agenda. In legislation supporting the Agriculture Act (Cap 318), the government created the HCDA to develop, promote, coordinate, and facilitate the horticultural industry in Kenya. Since then, direct government involvement in the subsector has been limited largely to issuing export licenses through HCDA. The government has not interfered in the marketing or distribution of crops, leaving these functions to the private sector.

The Agricultural (Export) Produce Act (Cap 319) provides for the grading and inspection of agricultural produce meant for export. A set of implementing rules ("the horticultural produce inspection rules") deals directly with horticultural produce destined for export from Kenya. In addition, the Standards Act (Cap 496) promotes the standardized specification of Kenyan commodities and ensures the implementation of a code of practice. This act provided for the establishment of the Kenya Bureau of Standards and the National Standards Council, entities that, in conjunction with the Kenya Plant Health Inspectorate Service, ensure that phytosanitary standards are adhered to by the industry. Compliance with standards keeps growers from spreading crop diseases and sending low-quality products into the market.

To ensure intellectual property rights, the Seeds and Plant Varieties Act (Cap 326) protects plant breeders for a period not exceeding 25 years. The Plant Variety Protection Office was established in Kenya in 1997 following the revision of the act in 1991. By 2004, a total of 640 applications had been received (Sikinyi 2004). Of these, 45 percent were presented by local breeders (mainly in food and industrial crops), while 55 percent were foreign applications mainly in horticultural crops. Eighty-eight percent were for ornamental crops (floriculture), representing more than 52 percent of all applications in Kenya. As a member of the International Union for the Protection of New Varieties of Plants, Kenya subscribes to the 1978 convention that provides for cooperation among member states in the sharing of data and information on variety testing and protection.

The establishment of the Kenya Industrial Property Office in February 1990, following the enactment of the Industrial Property Act (Cap 509), has strengthened intellectual property protection in Kenya. These developments have encouraged private research entities and breeders to operate in Kenya, as well as facilitated access to patented innovations and other international research outputs.

In the area of developmental policies (as communicated in so-called sessional papers and five-year development plans), Sessional Paper No. 1 of 1986 on "economic management for renewed growth" identified horticulture as one of seven priority commodities that the government was to focus on in order to achieve food security in the country.[6] In this paper, the government identified the key constraints facing horticultural development and committed itself to addressing these by building new marketing centers in major urban areas, according priority to products of high unit value in air shipment, experimenting with sea shipment, and improving market diversification. Noteworthy in this policy paper was the strengthening of HCDA and a redefinition of its roles to include providing technical advice to growers, collecting and disseminating market information, and providing specialized inputs such as refrigerated trucks for transportation.

Sessional Paper No. 1 of 1994 on "recovery and sustainable development to the year 2010" suggested steps for the government to take, including allocating land to private operators near the two international airports, installing precooling facilities at the international airports and in major growing areas, and maintaining jet fuel rates at competitive levels. The government divested its participation in the marketing and distribution of agricultural inputs and commodities. The paper also defined new research priorities and emphasized breeding programs for increased yield, disease and pest resistance, and research in integrated pest management. The need for timely, reliable information on available technologies, prices of inputs, and overseas markets was underscored. The paper states, in part, "that the research system and the extension service will be required to be up-to-date and highly responsive to farmers' needs."

Kenya's Poverty Reduction Strategy Paper of 2001 recognized the private sector as the engine of growth and limited the government's role in the economy, creat-

---

6. The other commodities were coffee, tea, pyrethrum, maize, wheat, milk, and meat products.

ing an enabling policy environment that encourages investment and job creation. The strategy also called for the development of a participatory extension and technology transfer system. This call for pluralism in extension services was further emphasized in the Economic Recovery Strategy for Wealth and Employment Creation (ERSWEC 2003–2007), which sought to consolidate the different acts of parliament governing agricultural activities into a single piece of legislation.

Besides an enabling policy and legal framework, various incentives are available to the cut flower industry in Kenya. Data from the Investment Promotion Council of Kenya show that investors in the cut flower industry can obtain tax allowances for capital investments including:

- Wear and tear on such items as trucks, tractors, computer hardware, copiers, motor vehicles, aircrafts, and plant machinery
- Industrial buildings
- Farm works, including all structures necessary for the proper functioning of a farm.

Exporting is promoted by manufacturing under bond schemes and export processing zones. The bond schemes target export businesses, while the EPZs provide import duty exemptions on imported inputs—a much more flexible export support program.

Both international and local seed companies ensure timely availability of certified seeds, planting materials, fertilizers, and other agrochemicals. The provision of cold storage, collection centers, precooling facilities, and refrigerated trucks in the major potential growing areas is an additional incentive to small-scale investors.

Key Success Factors

The success of Kenya's cut flower industry has been attributed to several factors—chief among them climatic conditions, other natural endowments, conducive policies, good infrastructure, and international trade arrangements.

Climate. Kenya enjoys a range of climatic conditions from the hot coastal plains to the cool highlands. A temperate climate prevails from 1,500 meters above sea level, with temperature ranges of 22–30 degrees Celsius during the day and 6–12 degrees Celsius at night. Rainfall is well distributed in the growing areas, with peaks in April–May and September–October covering approximately 60–80 days per year. This pattern allows for ample sunlight most of the year. These factors favor year-round cultivation and the export of high-quality flowers. The Lake Naivasha cluster, standing at an average of 1,850 meters above sea level, experiences a temperature range of between 7 and 23 degrees Celsius and an annual rainfall of 156 to 1,143 millimeters per month.

Other natural endowments. The key contextual factors responsible for the success of the Lake Naivasha cut flower cluster include the availability of huge tracts of land and freshwater resources both from Lake Naivasha and underground water resources. Land availability encouraged the initial investments in the area; today it continues to permit farms to expand. Flower growing is heavily dependent on irrigation; the availability of freshwater afforded by the lake ensures that irrigation can be done year-round.

An enabling policy environment. Both government support and lack of interference have been important factors in the industry's phenomenal growth. A fairly strong intellectual property protection regime, the availability of skilled manpower, functional quality-control and regulatory policies, and other government incentives have fostered the industry's rapid growth rate. The government's limited involvement in production and its hands-off approach to business operations have created space for strong private sector participation.

Infrastructure. The close proximity of major growing areas to the Jomo Kenyatta International Airport and the capital city of Nairobi, served by major airlines and charter operators, has not only minimized ground transportation costs but also provided air freight access into the European markets that account for the bulk of Kenya's flower exports.

Major growing areas are also served by major road networks; for example, the Lake Naivasha region is served by the Nairobi–Nakuru highway, the Thika region is served by Thika Road, and the Athi River and Kitengela areas are served by Mombasa Road. Feeder roads into the interior of growing regions still need upgrading, but the major roads provide easy access to the city center and airport.

Cooling facilities and refrigerated trucks, marketing centers in key growing areas, precooling facilities at the airports, and land allocated to private operators near airports constitute a supportive infrastructure for cut flower growers.

International trade agreements. The success of Kenya's cut flower industry has been largely attributed to its easy access to the European market. This is provided under the nonreciprocal preferential trade arrangements of the Lomé IV Convention, which allowed Kenya to export preferentially into the EU market. The Lomé IV Convention trade arrangement comes to a close at the end of 2007, to be replaced by a new trade arrangement being negotiated under the ongoing ACP–EU economic partnership agreements. The eclipse of the Lomé IV arrangements presents a big challenge to the cut flower industry, which is expected to face fierce competition from the neighboring countries of Ethiopia, Uganda, and Tanzania—all of which will still be classified as least developed countries.

Challenges Facing the Cluster

The Lake Naivasha cluster faces some major challenges.

Environmental pollution and resource depletion. Overdrawing of the lake's water for irrigation threatens the lake's existence. Munero (2004, quoted in Moturi, Polong, and Gitobu 2005) has stated that the horticultural farms of the lake region have encroached into riparian ecosystems, leading to pollution and overabstraction of lake waters. *The Daily Nation* (November 1, 2005) reported that the rapid extraction of water from Lake Naivasha for horticulture is putting the lake's existence at risk. The volumes abstracted have not been established (Gitahi 2005), but Becht and Harper (2002) have estimated an annual abstraction rate of $60 \times 10^6 \, m^3$. The water of the lake is believed to have receded from its former extent by some 700 meters in places. Moreover, the use of agrochemicals leads to an accumulation of chemical effluents, especially nitrates, that threaten aquatic life. Moturi, Polong, and Gitobu (2005) have reported that in recent years flower farms and fishermen around the lake have come into conflict over the diminishing number of fish in the lake, with the fishermen accusing the flower farms of overusing scarce water resources, thus reducing fish stocks.

Diseases and pests. Farms' close proximity makes it difficult to control the spread of infections.

Tension between local residents and flower farms. There have been complaints that formerly public beaches around the lake have been overtaken and privatized by flower farms and are no longer accessible to the public, thereby denying residents the use of these recreational facilities.

Key Lessons and Policy Implications

The case of the Lake Naivasha cluster presents several important policy-relevant lessons critical to the success of the cut flower industry in Kenya. These lessons are useful to other agricultural sectors that have experienced a decline in performance, both in Kenya and other parts of Africa. Most relate to the benefits of clustering.

Clustering accords farms, enterprises, and other actors in the sector an opportunity to interact, network, and collaborate with each other. This interaction, as Mytelka (2004) has argued, is an important stimulus for innovation and long-term competitiveness. The colocation of enterprises allows for a continual exchange of information, encouraging learning and the flow of knowledge. In the Lake Naivasha cluster specifically, farm owners consult each other on technological advancements, new varieties, market information, and regulatory requirements. Employees exchange valuable information on growing techniques, pest and disease management, and so forth. Through poaching and labor mobility, technology transfer and spillover occurs frequently. Staff mobility contributes to the cluster's overall functionality by promoting a mixing of ideas and allowing organizations to learn from each other.

Clustering promotes cooperation and a joint approach to problems facing the industry, increasing farmers' bargaining power. In addition to disseminating market intelligence to their members, industrial associations bargain on such matters as input prices and freight charges and lobby for policy support in infrastructure development and self-regulation in the areas of environmental, phytosanitary, and social health. This ensures a unified approach to issues affecting the industry.

By locating businesses in the same geographical area, clustering allows the government to provide well-targeted support to the industry. Development of infrastructure (roads, precooling facilities, cold stores), the establishment of regulatory offices, and pest and disease surveillance all become easier when dealing with a specific region.

Clustering facilitates subcontracting, marketing support, and technical assistance between large- and small-scale farms. Small farms can access export markets by selling through large farms, which in turn provide technical assistance to ensure good-quality flowers. These arrangements contribute to learning in the sector and help build the production capacity of small farmers. Subcontracting also enables large growers to supply their customers with varieties of flowers that they cannot produce on their own, either due to climatic factors or short-term demand.

Clustering also allows input suppliers and service providers easy access to a large number of farms and enterprises within a small geographic area. This reduces suppliers' operational and transportation costs, and is reflected in cheaper prices to farmers. The farmers can also organize themselves and purchase their inputs in bulk, further reducing the costs of farm inputs.

Conclusion

Markets, technologies, customers, and competitors are continually changing. Farms and enterprises must adapt and innovate in order to guarantee their competitiveness and sustainability. The case of the Lake Naivasha cut flower cluster demonstrates the usefulness of clustering in promoting technological learning, innovation, and competitiveness—resulting in increased productivity and export growth. The area's experience demonstrates that clustering creates opportunities for interaction and networking that are necessary if farms are to overcome the challenges and constraints facing industries in Africa. Networking within a cluster allows farms and enterprises to join forces around issues of common concern, and results in relationships with other independent actors to share knowledge, goods, and experiences while learning from each other with a common goal in mind (Engel 1997). Pinzas and Ranaboldo (2003), writing on the role of networking, argue that networks produce development only when they transform themselves into spaces of innovation, experimentation, and learning. This transformation requires strong links among the different organizations within the subsector, allowing for the exchange and transfer of information, technology, and resources.

Equally important to a cluster's overall effectiveness is the critical role of policies and incentives. A country's policy and legal framework determines corporate behavior, attitudes, and culture. A conducive environment promotes habits and practices that are beneficial to the industry. The availability of additional incentives and a favorable business environment has been significant in attracting private sector involvement and investment in the cut flower industry.

In general, sectoral specialization and geographic proximity result in the creation of a community of practice (Wenger 1997) within a cluster. These communities of practice are composed of sector practitioners who engage in joint activities and share information. Through sustained interaction, such communities develop a shared repertoire of resources including experiences, stories, tools, and ways of addressing recurring problems (Wenger 1997, 2005). In the Lake Naivasha cluster, as in Kenya's flower industry in general, these communities have taken the form of strong industrial associations such as the KFC and FPEAK, which tackle joint problems in markets, infrastructure, regulation, quality control, and lobbying.

References

Becht, R., and D. M. Harper. 2002. "Towards an Understanding of Human Impact upon the Hydrology of Lake Naivasha, Kenya." *Hydrobiologia* 488(1–3).

Bolo, M. 2005. "Agricultural Systems of Science, Technology and Innovation: The Case of Kenya's Floriculture Industry." To be published by the Technical Center for Agriculture and Rural Cooperation (CTA), The Netherlands.

Engel, P. G. H. 1997. *The Social Organization of Innovation, a Focus on Stakeholder Interaction.* Amsterdam: Royal Tropical Institute.

Gitahi, S. 2005. "Lake Naivasha: A Case of IWRM in Kenya." Available at www.netwas .org/newsletter/articles/2005/01/7

Kiptum, B. K. 2005. "Building Export Markets for Kenyan Flowers: Challenges and Opportunities Facing Small Scale Flower Growers in Kenya." Paper presented at the ATPS/ CTA national dissemination and exhibition workshop on the flower industry in Nairobi, Kenya, March 31, 2005.

Moturi, M. C. Z., F. Polong, and C. Gitobu. 2005. "The Distribution and Bioavailability of Heavy Metals in Sediments in Lake Naivasha, Kenya." An interim technical report submitted to the African Technology Policy Studies Network (ATPS) in November 2005.

Mytelka, L. 2004. "From Clusters to Innovation Systems in Traditional Industries." In B. L. M. Mwamila, L. Trojer, B. Diyamett, and A.K. Temu, eds., *Innovation Systems and Innovative Clusters in Africa*. Proceedings of a regional conference in Bagamoyo, Tanzania.

Pinzas, T. and C. Ranaboldo. 2003. *"La Union Hace la Fuerza? Estudio Sobre Redes en el Desarrollo Sostenible."* Lima and La Paz: ICCO.

Porter, Michael. 1990. *The Competitive Advantage of Nations.* New York: Basic Books.

Sikinyi, E. O. 2004. *"The Scope of Breeders' Rights in Kenya." Floriculture Magazine*, November/December. Nairobi, Kenya.

Wenger, Etienne. 1997. *Communities of Practice: Learning, Meaning and Identity.* Cambridge: Cambridge University Press.

———. 2005. "Communities of Practice: A Brief Introduction." Available on the Internet at www.ewenger.com/theory/communities_of_practice_intro.htm

5

The Nnewi Automotive Components Cluster in Nigeria

Boladale Oluyomi Abiola

Policies designed to support small and medium enterprises (SMEs) in Nigeria have a fairly long history. Various policy documents have highlighted the importance of SMEs in generating employment, raising incomes, and building the flexibility that allows industrial sectors to adapt to fluctuating demand patterns (Oyelaran-Oyeyinka, Adelaja, and Abiola 2005). SMEs in developing countries can grow and remain competitive through cluster formation. Clustering engenders collective efficiency, fostering external economies and joint actions that spur growth and competitiveness. By sharing resources, information, and technical knowledge, firms within a cluster help to reduce transaction costs. Most SME-related policies have proven ineffective, however, often because of poor implementation.

In this context, the emergence of a vibrant automotive components cluster in a remote part of rural southeastern Nigeria has attracted attention.[1] This cluster thrived even as a large swath of SMEs was closing down, unable to compete under newly produced governmental policies. And though Nnewi lacked essential infrastructure such as roads, water, and electricity, factory owners arranged for the private provision of these necessities (Brautigam 1997). Such policy and practical obstacles did little to stop the advance of industrial growth in the area.

Africa's automobile industry is one of the continent's fastest growing sectors, but it lacks the local technology needed to fully harness its potential to contribute to growth and development. This has meant that sector investment has been the preserve of a few automotive manufacturing companies, most based outside of the continent. Though it gained from strong long-distance relationships with Taiwanese companies (for machinery, equipment, and skills), the case of Nnewi is notable because its success has been driven by local initiatives and learning efforts. Nnewi remains an enclave based on strong kinship ties, relying on age-old apprenticeship methods and other informal institutions that in the beginning promoted trade and later fostered manufacturing activities.

---

1. The Nnewi cluster was introduced into policy discussion in Oyelaran-Oyeyinka (1997). That work also introduced the concept of clustering into Nigeria's policy environment. Materials for this chapter come from earlier research by Oyelaran-Oyeyinka (1997), updated in recent studies by Oyelaran-Oyeyinka, Adelaja, and Abiola (2005 and forthcoming). That work was revised for this volume by Boladale O. Abiola.

More than three decades old, the Nigerian automotive and component industry is is important to the national economy. Few industries allow for self-manufacturing, or use so many different raw materials, tools, machinery, and equipment. Consequently, the automotive industry serves as a stimulus for the development of other industries such as machine tool production, iron and steel, and transportation. Today, there are 12 automotive vehicle assembly plants, 5 of which are partially state-owned: Peugeot Automobiles Ltd., Lagos; Anambra Motor Manufacturing Co. Ltd., Anambra; Volkswagen Nigeria Ltd., Lagos; National Trucks Manufacturing Ltd., Kano; and Steyr Nigeria Ltd., Bauchi. The rest are privately owned. The automotive industry in Nigeria has a capacity to produce 102,000 cars, 55,000 commercial vehicles, 500,000 motorcycles, and 650,000 bicycles annually (*Info-Bulletin* 2002).

The focus of this chapter is the Nnewi automotive components cluster, which is made up of four villages—Otolo, Umudim, Uruagu, and Nnewichi. Each hosts a number of automotive spare parts manufacturing firms. Large and medium-size firms are generally located away from residential areas, while small enterprises are located in homes, apartment buildings, backyards, market stalls, and the federal government's Technology Incubation Centre. Colocation is evident; the question is whether the cluster generates enough collective efficiency and joint action to provide long-term benefits that can transform it into a center of innovation.

Cluster Profile

Nnewi is popularly known as the "Taiwan" or "Japan" of Africa. This is because of the high number of entrepreneurs who have built large, medium, and small factories at Nnewi, particularly for the manufacturing of automotive spare parts. Based on the number of employees, firms are classified as large (more than 50 employees), medium (10–49), small (2–9), and microenterprises (owner-operated) (table 5.1).

The development of the Nnewi automotive cluster can be traced to the dominance of the automotive spare parts market in Onitsha before the Nigerian civil war (1967–1970). With the destruction of Onitsha, rent costs soared. Most spare parts traders returned to Nnewi to sell in Nkwor Market. Social groupings, trading norms, and rules of cooperation evolved. Using the time-tested apprenticeship system, family members—and later, outsiders—were introduced into the trade. Through private savings, some traders became major importers of spare parts from Taiwan. It was from this class that the first Nnewi industrialists emerged between 1982 and 1992. They imported production technologies wholesale from product suppliers in Taiwan and trained Nigerian technicians either in-factory or in Taiwan (China). Among small entrepreneurs, it was common to start a business with manual or semi-automated tools, and only later to introduce advanced machinery.

Table 5.1. *Size distribution of automotive spare parts manufacturing enterprises in Nnewi*

	Number	Percent
Large	5	5.9
Medium	12	14.1
Small and micro	68	80.0
Total	85	100.0

Source: Oyelaran-Oyeyinka, Adelaja, and Abiola 2005.

A company like the Isaiah Nwafor Group was a major player in the importation of spare parts from Taiwan prior to 1983. The company later became Isaho Industries, Nnewi, and concentrated its efforts on producing aluminum alloys of various types and pistons for light generators, motorcycles, irrigation pumps, cars, and trucks. The Aluminum Smelting Company of Nigeria (ALUSCOM), Delta Steel, and the Ajaokuta Steel Company joined the effort, providing raw materials and molds. However, they could not produce the furnaces and crucible pots necessary, so Isaho Industries had to import these from Taiwan and, later, Mexico. The Nigerian Industrial Development Bank assisted the company in acquiring eight grinding machines from its trading partner in Taiwan. The Taiwanese partner trained six Nigerian employees and sent three Taiwanese nationals to transfer the technology. The technology transfer was mainly accomplished through apprenticeship, in-plant factory training, and learning by doing. At the peak of its manufacturing success in the mid-1990s, Nnewi was the source of more than 80 percent of motor spare parts in Nigeria.

This enclave of some 100,000 inhabitants has a long history. Nnewi has been the home of many illustrious businessmen specializing in trading and transportation. The story of the cluster follows the endeavors of traders and businessmen who made the remarkable transformation into manufacturers. Ventures into manufacturing started in the early 1980s and were made relatively easy because of entrepreneurs' extensive trading experience.

Most budding entrepreneurs have only an elementary education when they begin an apprenticeship, usually with help from a relative. There is a strong accent on kinship that defines the structure of both trading and manufacturing, particularly among small and medium entrepreneurs. The strategy is to keep skills and knowledge within the family, reducing the risk of losing a valuable worker. Consistent with other studies of SME clusters, trust between employers and employees is critical for success. Bringing relatives into the trading and manufacturing network reduces the risk of sabotage and ensures some measure of loyalty.

The Firms of the Nnewi Cluster

The pioneering study of the Nnewi cluster by Oyelaran-Oyeyinka (1997) focused on 17 firms engaged wholly or partly in automotive spare parts manufacturing, an area in which Nnewi firms have developed considerable skills and technical capabilities (table 5.2). Other manufactured products include motorcycle parts and components, cables and hoses, motorcycle engines and roller chains, automotive filters, and exhaust systems. All but a few of the firms are SMEs; all are fully Nigerian-owned. The same firms were studied in 2004 by Oyelaran-Oyeyinka, Adelaja, and Abiola (2005).

Scope and Methods of Research

A survey questionnaire supplemented by case studies of selected enterprises was used to collect the data for this study. The survey questionnaire contained both open- and close-ended questions intended to capture basic firm and owner characteristics, production and marketing performance, technological capabilities, networking and interfirm links, and the views of the firm owners on the existence and development of the clusters. The sample for the survey was made up of 17 firms that

Table 5.2. *Profile of firms in the Nnewi Cluster, 1997*

Firm	Firm size	Main products
1	Medium	Palm kernel mill; oil mill; bakery equipment
2	Medium	Motorcycle parts and components
3	Medium	Cables and hoses for automobiles
4	Medium	Motorcycle and motor engine roller chains
5	Small	Gears; motor bushings; machine sprockets; molds
6	Large	Auto and motorcycle batteries; spare parts
7	Large	Generator engines; auto and motorcycle parts; film-processing machines
8	Small	Motorcycle seats
9	Medium	Auto and motorcycle spare parts
10	Large	Automotive filters
11	Medium	Auto and motorcycle spare parts
12	Small	Machine spare parts
13	Medium	Power ropes; fan belts; industrial v-belts
14	Small	Feeder pillars; electrical equipment
15	Small	Exhaust systems
16	Small	Oil plant equipment; molds; hammer mills
17	Medium	Automotive spare parts

Source: Oyelaran-Oyeyinka, Adelaja, and Abiola 2005.
Note: All firms are Nigerian-owned.

were interviewed in 1997 and in 2004. In 2004 the number of firms was increased to 50 including the set of enterprises that was studied in 1997 except in cases where specific firms could not be found.

Technical Information

Close to 80 percent of the Nnewi firms are 10–20 years old. This shows that, in spite of Nigeria's economic difficulties, Nnewi businessmen have continued to invest in their firms, even during the years of the Structural Adjustment Program. Investment efforts include the widespread provision of private instrastructural facilities such as water boreholes, electricity-generating plants, and communication facilities. Ninety-eight percent of firms claim to maintain standby generator sets; 79.5 percent spend 1–20 percent of their total investment on power generators; and 12.8 percent spend 21–40 percent on private power generation. Small firms tend to spend a disproportionately large amount on utilities.

Our study focused on three key elements: the origin of investment in manufacturing technology, technological learning strategies, and the technological capabilities acquired.

Nnewi cluster firms share certain attributes that merit an in-depth investigation. These include:

- *Years in production.* Most were started just before or during the Structural Adjustment Program that began in 1986.

- *Ethnicity.* All are owned by entrepreneurs of Nnewi origin.
- *Background.* Almost all firm founders were illiterate or semiliterate traders who moved into manufacturing.
- *Origin of technology.* Practically all firms obtained their technology from Taiwan.
- *Uniform learning path.* Most entrepreneurs follow a general course from limited education, to trade apprenticeship, to trading, to manufacturing.
- *Success.* All cluster firms were doing well even when firms in other parts of Nigeria were folding up between the mid-1980s and early 1990s.

Sources of Equipment

Firms were asked to indicate what percentage of their equipment was imported (table 5.3). The majority of firms, close to 80 percent, imported between 61–100 percent of their total machinery. Some 52.6 percent imported 81–100 percent of machinery, while 26.3 percent of firms imported 61–80 percent of all their equipment from abroad. Only 21.1 percent fell into the 1–60 percent range.

Reasons for Investment and Technical Changes

The reasons for investing in new technology did not vary significantly with firm size. The majority of firms implemented technical changes simply to improve on old processes. Approximately 50 percent of all firms carried out innovations for this purpose (52.3 percent of small, 59 percent of medium, and 50 percent of large firms). However, while 50 percent of large firms invested to improve old *products*, only 16.3 percent and 20.4 percent of medium and small firms, respectively, did so. Seventy-five percent of large firms invested in innovations to produce a different variety of existing products. Some 22.5 percent of small enterprises and 18 percent of medium enterprises invested in expansion of plant capacity. This may indicate a significant potential for growth.

Our study investigated not only the direction of technical change, but the impetus for investing in a particular kind of activity. Of firms studied, 17.6 percent wanted to indigenize raw materials, 58.8 percent wanted "to achieve greater plant efficiency," while 23.5 percent were "responding to market pressures"; 83.3 percent of firms considered the changes "minor," while 16.7 percent thought they were "major." In-depth interviews with engineers in some of the enterprises revealed that while significant technical changes were being made, particularly in production, they qualified only as "modifications" to existing plant and equipment.

Table 5.3. *Foreign machinery imports*

Percent imported (%)	Percentage of importing firms
1–40	15.8
41–60	5.3
61–80	26.3
81–100	52.6

Source: Oyelaran-Oyeyinka, Adelaja, and Abiola 2005.

Table 5.4. *Rating of interfirm linkage types*

Type of linkage	Rating
Cooperation with local raw material suppliers	Average
Cooperation with foreign technical partners	High
Cooperation in sharing facilities	Average
Informal marketing and group purchasing abroad	Average
Cooperation with component suppliers abroad	High
Cooperation with domestic foundries and fabricators	Low
Subcontracting to produce intermediate and/or finished products	Low

Note: High – very close cooperation; Average – significant degree of cooperation; Low – not much cooperation (qualitative appraisal by the author).
Source: Oyelaran-Oyeyinka, Adelaja, and Abiola 2005.

Modes of Interfirm Networking

Firms within clusters exhibit different modes of interfirm linking. The nature and intensity of such networking vary according to the context and variety of firms in the cluster. The firms in the Nnewi sample engaged in the types of linkage shown in table 5.4. Foreign technological links currently form the primary basis for development, as indicated by the "high" ratings in the table.

Interfirm Learning and Collaboration

As firms interact in the cluster, they learn from one another. Internal and external economies of scale also affect their function, as do both vertical and horizontal links.

Horizontal links among SMEs. Horizontal cooperation among firms is still quite low (see table 5.5), particularly in the area of joint marketing (about 6.67 percent of respondents). However, over the five years from 1999 to 2004, there was a slight increase in the areas of information exchange and joint training. Generally, cooperation among firms has remained at consistent levels in most areas.

Backward links with subcontractors. The division of labor among firms and their subcontractors in the Nnewi cluster is still at a low level, except in the areas of information exchange and quality improvement. Cooperation levels with subcontractors have largely remained the same.

Backward links with input suppliers. The relationships between SMEs and suppliers seem to be improving, mainly in the areas of quality improvement and information exchange. More information is now available and circulates locally among firms and their input suppliers.

Forward links with domestic buyers. Our survey reveals that there is some cooperation in information exchange (50 percent) between Nnewi SMEs and domestic buyers. The highest level of cooperation is in quality improvement (72.23 percent of respondents). Of the total firms surveyed, 35.29 percent said they cooperate with domestic buyers in the standardizing of product specifications; 21.05 percent said they cooperate in the organization of their production.

Forward links with foreign buyers. Cooperation with foreign buyers is extremely low, particularly in the areas of information (85.77 percent) and joint labor training (85.71 percent). Only the areas of quality improvement and joint marketing show a very small increase in collaboration levels (accounting for 14.29 percent of total respondents).

Table 5.5. *Vertical and horizontal links among firms in the Nnewi cluster*

Cooperation among firms (percentage of firms reporting status of each form of cooperation)

	Strong increase	Increase	Remained same	Decrease	Strong decrease	Total
Exchange of information	11.1	16.7	50.0	11.1	11.1	100.0
Quality improvement	5.9	17.7	47.1	11.8	17.7	100.0
Joint labor training	11.8		58.8	11.8	17.7	100.0
Joint marketing	6.7		60.0	13.3	20.0	100.0
Backward cooperation with subcontractors						
Exchange of information	13.3	20.0	60.0	0.0	6.7	100.0
Technological upgrading	6.7	20.0	60.0	0.0	13.3	100.0
Quality improvement	13.3	20.0	60.0	0.0	6.7	100.0
Labor training	7.1		78.6	0.0	14.3	100.0
Joint marketing	7.1	7.1	71.4	0.0	14.3	100.0
Backward cooperation with input suppliers						
Exchange of information	13.3	20.0	53.3	6.7	6.7	100.0
Quality improvement	12.5	25.0	50.0	6.3	6.3	100.0
Speeding up delivery	11.8	5.9	58.8	17.7	5.9	100.0
Joint labor training	7.1	0.0	57.1	21.4	14.3	100.0
Joint marketing	7.1	7.1	57.1	14.3	14.3	100.0
Forward cooperation with buyers						
Exchange of information	27.8	22.2	38.9	5.6	5.6	100.0
Quality improvement	16.7	55.6	16.7	5.6	5.6	100.0
Setting of product specifications	23.5	11.8	58.8	0.0	5.9	100.0
Organization of production	5.3	15.8	57.9	0.0	21.1	100.0
Forward cooperation with foreign buyers						
Exchange of information	0.0	0.0	85.7	0.0	14.3	100.0
Quality improvement	0.0	14.3	71.4	0.0	14.3	100.0
Joint labor training	0.0	0.0	85.7	0.0	14.3	100.0
Joint marketing	0.0	14.3	71.4	0.0	14.3	100.0

Source: Oyelaran-Oyeyinka, Adelaja, and Abiola 2005.

Table 5.6. *Average number of employees per firm, by skill type, 2000–2004*

Staff category	2000	2001	2002	2003	2004
Management	2.20	2.20	2.50	2.50	2.83
Technical staff (local)	2.87	2.80	1.89	1.86	1.86
Technical staff (foreign)	0	3.00	5.00	4.00	4.00
Other unskilled	2.91	2.72	3.00	2.73	2.56
Total average	7.98	10.72	12.39	11.09	11.25

Source: Oyelaran-Oyeyinka, Adelaja, and Abiola 2005.

Knowledge and Technology in the Cluster

Entrepreneurs in the Nnewi cluster have a variety of educational backgrounds. The majority have a secondary school education (40.82 percent), followed by those with a technical education (28.75 percent). 16.33 percent of entrepreneurs held a university degree.[2] The Nnewi cluster has been able to provide employment opportunities to a great number of people who otherwise would have been jobless. Table 5.6 presents trends in average staff skills in the years 2000–04. Small enterprise development has been linked to employment generation (McCormick 1999). Small, informal activities generate employment for the growing number of men and women who cannot find work in agriculture, government service, or large-scale industry. Although many of the jobs provided by small firms are low-paying, they enable families to survive, educate their children, and—in some cases—move out of poverty.

The average number of employees per firm rose from 7.98 in 2000 to 12.39 in 2002 before dipping below 12 per firm in 2003 and 2004 (table 5.6). Technical management staff tend to dominate, constituting about 50 percent or more of total staff. It is interesting that foreign technical staff are more numerous than local. They numbered, on average, three per firm in 2001 (about 28 percent of the total staff), rising sharply to five per firm in 2002 (more than 45 percent of total staff) before declining to four per firm in 2003 and 2004 (when they constituted 43.4 percent and 42.6 percent of total staff, respectively).

The Nnewi cluster uses basic, necessary raw materials for its production activities from both local sources and abroad. More than 50 percent of SMEs reported that they use local inputs exclusively, while 6.12 percent reported using foreign raw materials. Meanwhile, 38.78 percent of firms reported that they used a combination of local and foreign inputs for their production activities.

Fifty percent of firms reported getting their core production machinery from both foreign and local sources; 38 percent get it solely from local sources; 12 percent import it exclusively from foreign countries. To solve major technical problems, 64 percent of firms still use local maintenance, while only 2 percent rely on foreign technical partners to solve their major problems. Evidently, there has been progress in building up domestic technical abilities.

---

2. These data are based on the 2005 survey and represents significant improvements in the educational attainment of owners. New owners of businesses with university degrees have begun to enter into the cluster, a contrast with the 1997 study where there was only one with a postsecondary degree.

Policy and Incentives

The government of Nigeria's involvement in the automotive industry dates back to the 1970s. The government hoped that building automotive assembly plants would boost engineering and other sectors of the economy by establishing a network of subcontracting firms and capabilities in local components and parts. However, 30 years after the modern Nigerian automotive industry took off, the pace of industry development is still very slow, particularly the development of local content. The government has had to create policies and incentives to revitalize the automotive industry and streamline and regulate its activities. This led to the establishment of the National Automotive Council in 1993. However, a number of indirect policies targeted at the manufacturing sector also seem to have considerably affected the automotive components subsector. These are discussed below.

The cluster enjoyed its golden age between 1986 and 1996. A turning point came with the Structural Adjustment Program of 1986–88 and its attendant devaluation of Nigerian currency, which made it difficult for firms to import spare parts and raw materials. But because several large-scale industrial projects (notably the Aluminum Smelting Company of Nigeria, Ikot Abasi, Delta Steel Company, and Aladja and Ajaokuta Steel) on which some of the Nnewi firms were supposed to rely for raw materials and production equipment never really got off the ground, the firms had to rely on expensive imports. Later, with globalization, Asian suppliers sent representatives to Nnewi to take spare parts orders directly from traders, drastically undercutting the prices of locally manufactured products.

These reasons may explain the closure of some of Nigerian factories, although other enterprises emerged. The closures included a number of small firms, some of which had served as suppliers to medium- and large-scale industries. Poor infrastructure, particularly in the supply of electricity and good roads, also had an impact. Frequent power outages caused large and medium-size firms to rely mainly on generators. Smaller firms that could not afford the cost of generators switched to manually operated equipment during such outages.

Our study examined the constraints on sources of raw materials (see figure 5.1). The constraints are measured on a Lickert scale of 1 to 5, with 1 representing the least constraining and 5 the most severe. A mean value of less than 2.5 means that the identified factor is not a major constraint. The major obstacles to procuring foreign inputs for the production of machinery and automotive components in the Nnewi cluster are high tariffs, limited sources of finance, custom formalities and duties, and insufficient information. Security has become a problem because of poor policing in industrial areas.

We also examined the effect of various direct and indirect government policies (such as tax incentives, grants, regulations) on the Nnewi firms. Most firms perceived government support as weak, with less than 7 percent of firms calling it strong in any given area (table 5.7).

Public goods support was also seen as inadequate. Of physical infrastructure elements, only telephone and Internet services were rated good (figure 5.2). Improvements in telephone and Internet services may be related to the introduction of GSM Phone into the country in 2001, which has increased the country's telephone density tremendously. More than 50 percent of firms agreed that basic infrastructure was very poor. The most problematic element is electricity supply; 70 percent of firms rate it poorly. Other important facilities such as water and transports also receive low ratings.

Figure 5.1. Constraints faced by firms in the importation of components

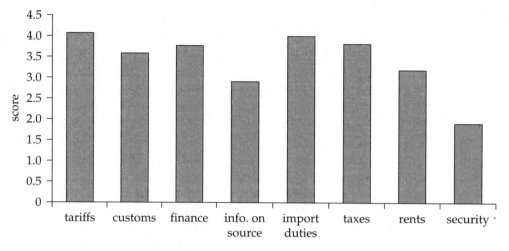

Note: The higher the score, the more serious the constraint posed by a factor.
Source: Oyelaran-Oyeyinka, Adelaja, and Abiola 2005.

Table 5.7. Firms' perception of government support to the cluster

	Innovation	Available skilled manpower	University support	R&D	Intellectual property protection	IT support	Venture capital
Weak support	89.8	77.1	89.4	93.8	87.5	91.1	95.7
Good support	8.2	16.7	10.6	6.3	10.4	8.9	2.1
Strong support	2.0	6.3	0.0	0.0	2.1	0.0	2.1
Total	100.0	100.0	100.0	100.0	100.0	100.0	100.0

Source: Oyelaran-Oyeyinka, Adelaja, and Abiola 2005.

Figure 5.2. Firms' assessment of physical infrastructure

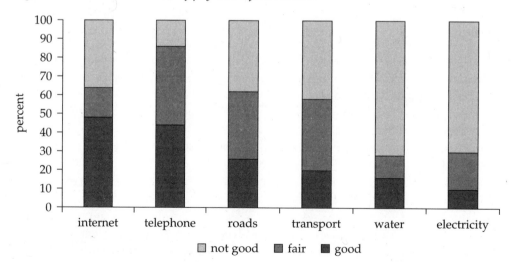

Source: Oyelaran-Oyeyinka, Adelaja, and Abiola 2005.

In the absence of effective municipal and state support, the role of trade and manufacturing associations has been crucial. Two private industry associations are fairly active: the Nnewi Chamber of Commerce, Industry, Mines and Agriculture, which is dominated by large- and medium-scale manufacturing firms, and the Nigerian Association of Small Scale Industries. The associations are organized to articulate the needs, challenges, and plans of their member enterprises to governments at different levels. They provide advice and information on export destinations, on government policies, and so forth.

Creating an Enabling Environment—An Unmet Policy Challenge

The government of Nigeria has not created an enabling environment for the development of an efficient and dynamic manufacturing sector. Inconsistencies in macroeconomic policies, an unreliable electricity supply, and the absence of a clustering policy that targets a local economy such as Nnewi undermine the sector's dynamism.

Throughout Nigeria, entrepreneurs have to contend with a very high-risk business environment. Apart from poor infrastructure, property rights are poorly specified and often difficult to enforce; numerous regulations have to be dealt with, which is costly in terms of both time and money (for bribes). More generally, poor market information significantly raises transaction costs. Transaction costs are high in part because the state has not provided the kinds of public goods that would reduce them.

What is special about the Nnewi business community is that in both formal and informal institutions, patterns of behavior have evolved that lower transaction costs in a variety of ways. Eastern Nigeria is the home of Igbo culture, the well-recognized characteristics of which (individualism, competitiveness, and receptivity to change) fuel entrepreneurialism and capitalism in the region. Igbos invest heavily in education and training, and rules of inheritance encourage specific institutional factors that have played a central role in facilitating industrial development in Nnewi.

During the early stages of Nigeria's short-lived economic reform program, which lasted from 1986 to 1992, manufacturing enterprises responded very positively to improved incentives and input availability. The industrial boom in Nnewi predated this reform, and cluster activities were sustained well into the 1990s, when much of the rest of the manufacturing sector in Nigeria was crippled by foreign exchange shortages, rapidly deteriorating infrastructure, and depressed domestic demand (Bennell 1998).

The role of informal institutions in substituting for the state has been important to the growth of the sector. Numerous cultural practices lower transaction costs in Nnewi. For example, trading networks have engendered a form of cooperative competition that has been transferred to manufacturing. In particular, the sharing of equipment and lending of skilled personnel is common. Close, trust-based relationships also ensure that key information travels quickly among producers and traders. Furthermore, Nnewi entrepreneurs have developed close links over the years with spare parts producers and wholesalers in Taiwan and other Asian countries. These links proved to be especially valuable when Nnewi traders began to develop their own production activities. They obtained detailed advice and other technical assistance from their Asian suppliers about the type of machinery and

Table 5.8. Assessment of the competitive environment

	Faster delivery time	Packaging quality	Conformity to standards	Price	Product quality
Less demanding	11.1	0.0	5.9	5.9	8.3
Remain same	50.0	35.3	47.1	52.9	0.0
More demanding	38.9	64.7	47.1	41.2	91.7
Total	100.0	100.0	100.0	100.0	100.0

Source: Oyelaran-Oyeyinka, Adelaja, and Abiola 2005.

other technologies they should acquire and the specific skills needed to operate efficiently (Brautigam 1997).

Liberalization, Government, and the Competitive Challenge

The Nnewi cluster is faced with considerable competition from Asian countries. Three-quarters of the firms surveyed consider these countries' imports to be severely affecting their operations. In general, firms indicated that the competitive environment in the past five years had been very demanding in virtually all areas that dictate competition in the industry see (table 5.8).

In order to remain competitive, firms in the cluster have devised various strategies. However, the lack of strong public goods undermines firm-level efforts. This is a major lesson for the Nigerian government. Industrial dynamism is dependent on overall public policy and requires the provision of public goods. The main competitive advantage of Asian firms is price. Nnewi firms have been unable to match the lower prices of Asian goods. Their main hope is to increase the quality of their products and their reliability in the delivery of their products to customers. To achieve these objectives, the cluster requires the support of the government.

References

Bennell, P. 1998. "Industrial Restructuring in Africa during the 1990s: Outcomes and Prospects." University of Sussex, Sussex, United Kingdom.

Brautigam, D. 1997. "Substituting for the State: Institutions and Industrial Development in Eastern Nigeria." *World Development* 25 (7):1063–1080.

Info-Bulletin. 2002. "Engineering Export." *Info-Bulletin* 12 (11). Nigeria Weekly

McCormick, D. 1999. Value Chains, Production Networks and the Business System, Discussion Notes Prepared for the Value Chains Workshop, organized by the Rockefeller Conference Centre, Bellagio, Italy. September 25–October 1, 1999.

Oyelaran-Oyeyinka, B. 1997. *Nnewi: An Emergent Industrial Cluster in Nigeria.* Ibadan, Nigeria: Technopol.

Oyelaran-Oyeyinka, B., M. Adelaja, and B. O. Abiola. 2005. "Small and Medium Enterprise Clusters in Nigeria." Unpublished paper funded by UNU-MERIT, Maastricht.

Oyelaran-Oyeyinka B., and D. McCormick, eds. 2007 (forthcoming). *Industrial Clusters and Innovation Systems in Africa: Learning Institutions and Competition.* Tokyo: United Nations University Press.

6

The Otigba Computer Village Cluster in Nigeria

Boladale Oluyomi Abiola

Conventional wisdom suggests that poor countries are unlikely to host the production of high technology, particularly within small and medium enterprises (SMEs). Significantly, the evolution of the Otigba Computer Village in Lagos, Nigeria, has proceeded largely without direct support from the state, and, indeed, within a decidedly hostile institutional environment bereft of solid infrastructure.[1]

The Otigba Computer Village exhibits two features of clustering that could potentially transform it into a local innovation system producing high-value products. Its emerging firm-level capabilities in assembling computer hardware (a complex product[2]) and its growing interfirm interactions have the potential to form an enduring knowledge-based cluster. More significantly, Otigba exhibits a pattern of development found in local economies that have made successful transitions into modern production.

The major activity in the cluster is the assembly and trading of computers and peripherals.[3] This activity offers a low-risk approach to rapid technological advance for two reasons (Kash, Auger, and Li 2004). First, it thrives on incremental innovation because the basic technological design has been established and the uncertainty attending later innovations has been largely eliminated. Second, the technological infrastructure required is established and can support greater autonomous domestic innovation efforts that extend beyond the initial products.

The Otigba Computer Village exemplifies the possibilities of a high-tech cluster in an African setting, a phenomenon unique among the numerous small and micro enterprises in low-tech sectors in Africa. The cluster provides employment

---

1. This chapter summarizes a research project reported in greater detail by Oyelaran-Oyeyinka (2006) and Abiola (2006).
2. A good is categorized as *complex* if either the good itself or the process of manufacturing it is complex. A complex technology, unlike a simple technology, such as furniture making or footwear, requires the support of organizational forms, whereas the latter can be understood by an individual. Complex goods are different from high-tech ones in that the latter are measured by the ratio of R&D expenditure to output. See United Nations, *Statistical Year Book of International Trade*.
3. Building a local system of production and innovation is a path followed by arguably the most successful computer industry based on the clustering of SMEs in the developing world (Mathews 2006). Taiwan's computer industry has relied on extensive imports of components and parts from Japan, reflecting of the pronounced global division of labor in the industry.

not only to low-skilled traders of computer components but also to high-skilled labor, including owners of enterprises who are graduates of university programs in electronic engineering and computer science. Between 55 and 60 percent of the entrepreneurs in the Otigba Computer Village are university graduates.

How does a cluster like this grow and prosper in the absence of direct state support, and, more importantly, in the absence of solid infrastructure and public goods?

Scope and Method of Research

The Otigba Computer Village, also known as the Ikeja Computer Village, is located in Ikeja, the industrial center of Lagos. The former capital city of Nigeria, Lagos is a sprawling set of towns with a population of more than 7 million. It is the commercial center of the nation and home to many industries, government agencies, the head offices of most financial institutions, embassies of other countries, and many commercial institutions. It has Nigeria's major seaport and busiest international airport. Lying in the heart of Ikeja, the cluster is bordered by Unity Road, Awolowo Road, and Oba Akran Avenue. It has been variously described as the information and communication technology (ICT) hub of West Africa, potentially the biggest ICT market in Africa, and the Silicon Valley of West Africa. With an area of 325 square kilometers (Bamiro 2003), the cluster comprises eight streets, with Otigba being the most popular because of its size and the volume of business activities carried out there daily. The activities in the Otigba Computer Village involve the sales, service, and repair of ICT products and components. A core group of firms is involved in the production of systems cloned from imported components.

Our study evaluated enterprise size capacity, development, modes of operation, performance, and sustainability. We also analyzed factors constraining cluster growth.

Both primary and secondary data were collected. The primary data were obtained through questionnaires; secondary data were gathered through a participatory research appraisal using a structured interview guide. The information gathered included input sources, technology (both process and product) sources, infrastructure availability, level of technical and financial support, market access, and the level of cluster collaboration.

More than 3,500 enterprises are registered with the Computer and Allied Products Association of Nigeria (CAPDAN). In addition, street operators number about 1,500. Four hundred fifty questionnaires were administered randomly to ensure that those who keep more than two or three outlets in the cluster were not interviewed twice. The involvement of CAPDAN officers was crucial to the success of the survey, particularly in encouraging its members to respond to the questionnaire. Lack of response from enterprise owners had been an obstacle in the early stages of our study.

Cluster Profile

The Otigba Computer Village began trading imported ICT equipment, components, and products more than 12 years ago. The cluster began in a residential area with a handful of shops along Otigba and Pepple streets. Over time, the cluster grew to become a beehive of computer hardware and software trade and production. The stimulus for its growth was the relatively high demand for computers and peripherals from businesses and academic institutions—Lagos is home to 60 percent of Nigeria's industrial production and the region also has the nation's highest percentage of educated people and educational institutions. Two periods can be identified in the evolution of the Otigba Computer Village.

Stationery and Office Equipment Sales

The cluster began in the early 1990s with a few sales and repair outlets specializing in stationery, printers, photocopiers, branded computers, and office equipment.

The two major streets on which the cluster developed were originally designed and approved as a residential area. But the quiet neighborhood turned into a major business district. As demand for computers grew, Otigba Street, the longest in the district, quickly assumed the agglomerative character of a cluster. By 1998, most of the residential buildings had been converted into new high-rise shopping complexes. Increased activity in the computer and information technology (IT) sectors in Otigba and its environs led to the development of a knowledge-based cluster that has not encouraged the entry of new enterprises and generated employment for university graduates.

As new IT businesses grew, space became scarce and new business buildings were constructed, largely through private efforts.[4] This singular act brought the previously unrecognized computer components and accessories business in Lagos into the national limelight, but still did not elicit positive support from local and state governments. The cluster was characterized by a wide range of computer hardware and peripherals, which ushered in a new generation of computer hardware assembly and allied IT businesses in Nigeria.

Computer Assembly

By 2002–03, the Otigba ICT cluster held about 2,500 sales and repair outlets dispersed across the cluster. In full operation, the cluster had started to attract entrepreneurs, and the locale changed significantly. New actors included retailers, importers of computers, and, notably, builders of computer clones, many of them SMEs (figure 6.1). The retail market changed to include more activities such as the direct importation of computer parts (which previously had been limited to a few privileged firms). Emerging business activities included the direct sale, repair, and servicing of computers and all kinds of office equipment and accessories. The popular *Tokunbo*[5] business cuts across every sector of the economy in Nigeria, and the Otigba cluster has been a hub of computer imports. The sale of used imported computers, and refurbished old ones, is as common as the sale of new products.

---

4. Notable among this is the Police Women's Association (POWA) shopping complex with 100 office spaces at 30/31 Otigba street. This initiative stimulated the entrepreneurial spirit of vendors of computers and allied products.
5. *Tokunbo* is an ethnic Yoruba word meaning "imported." The term has assumed a specific business meaning to denote the importation of second-hand electronic goods, components, and parts, and motor vehicle parts. Second-hand consumer goods and appliances, as well as industrial machinery and replacement parts, have become a multibillion dollar business in Nigeria, although precise figures are not available.

Figure 6.1. *Small and medium-size enterprises in the Otigba Computer Village cluster*

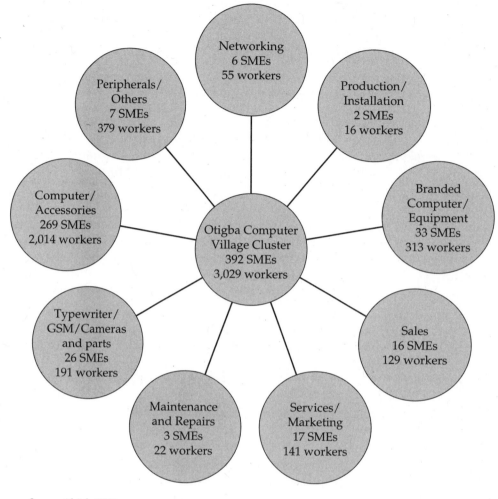

Source: Abiola 2006.

Within the past five years, and through the individual efforts of vendors and operators, the Otigba Computer Village has transformed itself into an international ICT market that serves not only Nigerian demand, but also countries in the West African subregion and elsewhere in the continent, as the cluster has attracted buyers and traders from neighboring African countries. By the end of 2003, the cluster had grown in size and undergone a major structural change—it now included more computer shopping malls and street software vendors. By the end of 2005, the cluster was home to some 5,000 medium, small, and microenterprises that directly employed about 10,000 people. Box 6.1 illustrates the typical path of an entrepreneur into the cluster. Recently, bigger players from the formal sector have begun to arrive as well.[6]

With the growth of business, more financial institutions and banks have moved into the cluster (or nearby) to take advantage of the high volume of money gener-

---

6. "It is the place to be now or you go under," noted an IT hardware company executive relocating to the cluster from the highbrow part of Lagos.

Box 6.1. *Entrepreneurship trajectory at Otigba Computer Village*

The case of Victor, the managing director of Rofem Cybernetics, illustrates the typical trajectory and entrepreneurial spirit of the owners of the highly innovative enterprises in the Otigba Computer Village cluster. Victor received his first degree in business administration from the Ahmadu Bello University, Zaria, Nigeria, in 1999. He purchased his first computer when he was an undergraduate student. Dissatisfied with the performance of his laptop and curious about the technology, he started pulling the system apart and reassembling the various components based on his reading of computer manuals and publications. He gained confidence and became a self-taught expert. Having upgraded his laptop, he sold it to one of his lecturers. This singular sale unexpectedly started him on his journey into the computer business. The news of the sale made him popular with other lecturers, who approached him, asking him to supply them with similar systems. To satisfy this initial demand, he traveled to Lagos (a distance of about 800 kilometers from Zaria) to shop for lightly used and serviceable laptops. With the unexpected increase in demand for computers in the university, Victor says, "I had no alternative but to establish a computer sale and service shop in Zaria and hire a few people to help me in its operation since I was still an undergraduate. The shop still exists and has grown."

After graduation, Victor moved to Lagos and enrolled in a short course in e-Technology at NIIT, an international IT training outfit. This sharpened his technical skills in computer software, hardware repair, and servicing, particularly for the more intricate laptops and notebooks. Victor remembers, "At this point I faced the dilemma of either accepting a fairly good job offer from a bank or launching fully into the computer business. I chose the latter and came to the Otigba cluster to establish Rofem Cybernetics as a computer sales and service enterprise with specialization in notebooks and laptops of all brands."

With a staff of 10, Victor has been closely following developments in computer technology. He has been moving from a notebook sales and service operation to assembling his own brand of notebooks using imported parts and components, with casings and keyboards manufactured by a company in Asia based on his design. His company has several clients both within and outside Nigeria, including Benin, Senegal, Kenya, and the Republic of Congo.

Source: Oyelaran-Oyeyinka 2006.

---

ated by the rapid economic development of the area. Growth has has also brought the hustle and bustle of buyers and eager sellers and the ever-present human and automobile traffic congestion along the streets leading into the market.

Compared with traditional clusters in Africa, a notable characteristic of the Otigba cluster is the level of interfirm cooperation and joint action, both of which developed in response to poor state support and sometimes hostile municipal government policy. Both have fostered growth. Much of the cooperative competition is mediated by CAPDAN. Established in 2003, this organization has gained legitimacy as an umbrella association addressing challenges to its membership in the areas of technology and market support, security, and infrastructure maintenance.[7]

---

7. According to the present president of CAPDAN, Mr. Ibrahim Tunji Balogun of Balog Technologies Ltd., the number of cluster enterprises registered with the association is over 3,500, with the employees numbering between 8,000 to 10,000, excluding their employers. There is an estimated minimum turnover on individual investment of over 5 million naira per annum ($30,000). This is the mean for much of the small operators. There are instances where some of the enterprises realize these figure in a week.

Table 6.1. *Changes in competitive factors (percent)*

	Less demanding	Remained same	More demanding	Total
Faster delivery time	4.05	37.07	58.89	100
Packaging quality	5.80	35.07	59.13	100
Conformity to standards	14.29	21.57	64.14	100
Price	11.35	25.87	62.79	100
Product quality	8.37	18.06	73.57	100

Source: Oyelaran-Oyeyinka (2005).

The high level of cooperation is also attributable to the number of educated entrepreneurs with ties to schools; though otherwise strangers, they have bonded together to face the common threats of fierce competition and poor state support. There is, as well, a surprising amount of cooperation among small emerging enterprises and the bigger IT operations within the cluster. In this atmosphere, a new competitive market structure has emerged with a free flow of price information, technological support, and major market strategy information. Otigba Computer Village has produced many trained personnel, some of whom are now self-employed within the cluster; others have set up businesses outside, even while maintaining links with cluster businesses for procurement and technical support.

Collective action within the cluster also is evident in the form of interfirm credit facilities,[8] joint technical support (knowledge sharing), joint warehousing in response to limited space in the cluster, and active membership in CAPDAN.

In addition to local market competition, a major impetus for cooperation is the fierce threat posed by imports from outside Africa, particularly China, Malaysia, and Dubai. Trade liberalization has brought a considerable change in the competitive environment. Major factors of increased competition include the duration of product delivery, product and packaging quality, price, and conformity to standards. These changes have been demanding for enterprises in the cluster, and firms have employed different strategies to remain competitive (table 6.1); in all of these, they have benefited from the cluster's agglomeration of firms.

Since the competitive environment has become more demanding, firms have embarked on different activities to increase the sale and quality of their products. The main approaches are price reductions made possible by intelligent sourcing and aggressive promotion to create product awareness and convince prospective buyers of the quality they will be getting for their money. In addition, sales promotions, better equipment, and staff incentives have been mobilized to improve product quality. Other local market strategies deployed by operators include enhanced distribution networks and good customer service.

---

8. One way the informal credit arrangements work is between large and small enterprises, where the former supplies goods to the latter on credit for an agreed period of time. These kinds of interfirm collaborations have been necessary because the banks rarely lend to small firms. The system works because most of the entrepreneurs belong to the same social networks.

Table 6.2. Staffing trends in Otigba cluster, 2000–2004

Average number of employees of firms

	2000	2001	2002	2003	2004
Management staff	2.5	2.7	2.8	2.8	2.8
Local technical staff	2.5	2.5	2.5	2.7	2.8
Foreign technical staff	1.0	0.9	0.9	0.7	0.9
Other unskilled	2.5	2.6	2.8	3.1	3.2
Average total	6.1	6.4	6.9	7.6	7.6

Source: Oyelaran-Oyeyinka 2006.

In today's globalized economy, inputs into the production process are sourced locally and internationally so as to produce products at a highly competitive price. Enterprises in the Otigba Computer Village source locally but also reach out to global players. Local sources account for an average of 36.5 percent of all inputs used in the cluster, with foreign inputs composing the rest. The products imported into the cluster depend on the nature of the importing business. Products may be components, finished products, or both; 26 percent of firms import finished goods only, while 13 percent import components only. The remaining 61 percent import both components and finished products.

Since imported products account for more than two-thirds of the components and finished products available in the cluster, it is safe to say that firm performance is dependent on the ease of importation.

Entrepreneurs also have responded to increased competition from abroad by establishing technical and production channels with firms in these countries. This has led to an increase in informal exportation and importation, with price being the major factor.[9]

The average size of firms in the cluster has increased over time. Cluster firms had an average of six employees in 2000. That number increased to nearly eight by 2003 (table 6.2).

Knowledge and Technology Aspects of the Cluster: Interfirm Learning and Collaboration

As we have previously discussed, a unique feature of the cluster is the presence of a large number of highly skilled and educated graduates in electronics, computer sciences, and related disciplines. Tacit knowledge is diffused through apprenticeship.

Interfirm collaboration has raised the cluster's collective competitiveness. As noted earlier earlier, that collaboration has been made possible by the educated vendors and operators within the cluster. Fifty-five percent of study respondents are university graduates, 15 percent are graduates of polytechnic institutes, 20 percent are technicians, and the remaining 10 percent are unskilled traders.

---

9. Informal exports and imports are transborder trade not recorded in a country's trade data. Visitors to Nigeria from other countries in the region often purchase goods in small quantities for use or resale at home. Such goods typically pass over the Nigerian border unrecorded.

Otigba provides a promising example for the development of small-scale enterprises in Nigeria. Our findings reveal that 88 percent of the enterprises are wholly owned by Nigerians, while only 10 percent are wholly owned by foreigners. The remaining 2 percent are joint ventures between Nigerians and foreigners. Entrepreneurship tends to be driven by the education levels of entrepreneurs. More than 90 percent of the entrepreneurs have formal schooling beyond the secondary school level. While 62 percent of these owners have education up to the university level, an additional 30 percent have technical education after their secondary education. This is very important, given that the computer business is highly technical and requires considerable knowledge and skills.

The strength of clusters lies in the quantity and quality of the interfirm learning collaboration among members. Collaboration generates positive externalities that reduce average transaction costs—a benefit that individual enterprises may not be able to generate by themselves. Lack of cohesiveness, by contrast, can limit the capacity of SMEs to defend their collective interests and effectiveness. Interfirm links, whether horizontal or vertical, determine overall cluster performance and can ultimately improve competitiveness on a large scale. Our findings reveal that cooperation is prevalent in the Otigba Computer Village. More than 97 percent of the enterprises studied indicate that they cooperate with other firms within the cluster, while 78 percent and 99 percent of the enterprises collaborate in subcontracting and in the activities of industrial associations, respectively.

Our study examined the changing horizontal and vertical links among enterprises. Starting with horizontal links, firms reported a tremendous increase in their level of cooperation with other firms, and no firm indicated a strong decrease. This also translated into greater use of industrial associations. The industrial associations were formed to foster unity and embed social capital that can be tapped by members. Although 19 percent of firms indicated that they saw no change in this relationship over the past five years, 76 percent of the firms indicated that there had been an increase in the use of industrial associations (table 6.3). Most of the horizontal links identified are in joint marketing, quality improvement, and information exchange; 87 percent, 83 percent, and 80 percent of firms, respectively, indicated that their interfirm links in these areas had increased over the past five years. However, a significant percentage of the enterprises had not increased their collaboration with other firms. For example, in the case of joint labor training, 26.9 percent of the enterprises indicated that their efforts in this area had remained the same over the last five years.

There is evidence of considerable vertical links, of which there are two main types: forward and backward. Evidently, firms in the cluster engage in two main types of backward links: collaboration and cooperation with suppliers and contractors. There is considerable cooperation between firms and suppliers and contractors in all areas of operation, including information exchange, quality improvement, and so on. But little industry–university linking can be discerned, except through the continuous supply of engineering graduates. Weak links in this area are due in part to the well-known isolation of universities from enterprises at this level of development; academics traditionally conceptualize their role in terms of R&D, which is of little relevance to this class of enterprise. More importantly, there is little policy pressure to foster such collaboration.

The same is true for collaboration with buyers, both domestic and foreign. More than 80 percent of the firms indicated that in the past five years, cooperation had

Table 6.3. *Firms' perceptions of changing horizontal and vertical links (percent)*
Percentage of firms reporting degree of change in various forms of linkage

	Strong increase	Increase	No change	Decrease	Strong decrease	Total
Cooperation with other firms	41.61	50.67	7.38	0.34	0.00	100
Use of industrial associations	19.73	56.12	19.73	3.74	0.68	100
Horizontal links						
Exchange of info. and experience	31.37	49.02	16.99	2.61	0.00	100
Quality improvement	29.09	54.18	14.55	2.18	0.00	100
Joint labor training	18.65	43.65	26.98	8.73	1.98	100
Joint marketing	35.49	51.54	11.73	0.93	0.31	100
Backward links with input suppliers						
Exchange of info. and experience	32.48	53.7	13.83	0.00	0.00	100
Quality improvement	24.14	67.24	8.28	0.00	0.34	100
Speeding up delivery	30.69	51.38	14.83	3.1	0.00	100
Joint labor training	17.04	38.52	31.48	10.74	2.22	100
Joint marketing	40.26	44.73	10.86	3.83	0.32	100
Backward links with subcontractors						
Exchange of info. and experience	22.63	60.95	15.69	0.73	0.00	100
Technological upgrading	22.09	58.53	18.99	0.39	0.00	100
Quality improvement	20.77	59.62	18.46	0.77	0.38	100
Labor training	16.47	40.96	31.33	10.04	1.2	100
Joint marketing	35.23	46.26	13.52	2.14	2.85	100
Forward links with main buyers						
Exchange of info. and experience	53.27	42.68	4.05	0.00	0.00	100
Quality improvement	38.13	48.44	13.44	0.00	0.00	100
Setting up of product specifications	36.24	50.00	10.4	3.36	0.00	100
Organization of production	23.16	46.67	26.67	3.16	0.35	100
Forward links with foreign buyers						
Exchange of info. and experience	31.03	58.62	10.00	0.34	0.00	100
Quality improvement	21.45	60.73	16.73	1.09	0.00	100
Joint labor training	23.11	30.28	33.86	8.37	4.38	100
Joint marketing	26.64	50.19	20.08	2.32	0.77	100

Source: Oyelaran-Oyeyinka 2006.

increased tremendously between them and the buyers of their products. The lowest form of cooperation exists in joint labor training with foreign buyers; even in that case cooperation has increased in more than 53 percent of firms.

Export Activities

Exporting usually raises the level of firm capability, driving firms to pay attention to quality as well as price. Intense competition with larger-sized firms and manufacturing brands, as well as with importers, has been a source of cluster competitiveness. Our findings show that 50.2 percent of the firms in Otigba are engaged in export activities. Formal exports are made by 47.5 percent, while informal exports are made by 52.5 percent of enterprises. In addition, 40.7 percent of small-scale enterprises and 53.6 percent of medium-scale enterprises are engaged in exporting. Though Nigerian producers face enormous challenges from Asian countries, competition has opened up opportunities to explore other markets in the subregion. Enterprises have used different methods to reach export markets. The most prominent is selling to overseas buyers who come to Nigeria. This is followed by the process of selling to domestic export agents, who in turn export the goods. There are also occasions where the enterprises export directly to clients overseas or to overseas agents.

Policy and Incentives

Nigeria has enacted a National Information Technology Policy document relevant to ICT activities in the Otigba Computer Village. The document specifies policies in areas that include:

- Promotion of alliances and partnerships among local firms, as well as with foreign firms through the establishment of joint ventures and strategic alliances based in tax-free technology parks.
- Duty-free importation of IT components and software tools for the sole purpose of exporting finished IT products and services.
- A 1.5 percent import duty on "knocked down" (unfinished) IT components for the domestic market, as opposed to a 7.5 percent import duty on imported finished IT goods for the domestic market.
- Tax holidays for all enterprises that demonstrate substantial financial commitment to the advancement of IT capacity and staff training.
- Federally owned, funded, or controlled organizations need not deduct statutory withholding taxes from payments to Nigerian IT solutions providers for the following services, among others:
  - 100-percent locally developed software
  - Locally assembled or manufactured ICT equipment
  - Internet access services, local Web hosting, and local Web sites

In addition, government establishments have been directed to use locally assembled computers. This policy has helped local actors in the formal and informal sectors of the economy. The government policy is two-pronged: one, increasing patronage to create markets for local products, and, two, creating a tariff structure to favor local production. The two policies that have been the most effective are state procurement and tariff reduction on imported components.

Table 6.4. *Prominent features of the Otigba Computer Village cluster*

- A strong entrepreneurial culture that enables the cluster to grow despite obstacles.
- Cooperative competition in which actors compete but remain involved in joint action.
- A relatively strong skill base, necessary for knowledge-based activities.
- Growth and innovation in response to changing market demands.
- Significant cross-border trading in IT products as the cluster emerges as the IT hub of West Africa.
- Very high capacity for employment generation, mainly in the form of apprenticeships.
- Synergy between the trading activities in computer components and allied products on the one hand, and the computer-assembly operations that involve these traded items.
- Heavy reliance on imports of computers, components, and peripherals, making the cluster sensitive to macroeconomic variables such as foreign exchange and import duties.
- Negotiated settlements with major software copyright holders brokered by the cluster's association.

Key Success Factors

The major factors accounting for the success of the Otigba cluster have already been discussed. They are summarized in table 6.4. Chief among them is the strong, cooperative entrepreneurial culture that enables the cluster to grow despite weak or nonexistent institutional support, poor infrastructure (especially electricity, roads, and available buildings), and a shortage of long-term project financing that obliges operators to rely on internally generated resources for project implementation.

The collective technical capability of the cluster in computer servicing, repair, and system design is a major factor behind the cluster's success. The collective IT capabilities that exist in this cluster are at a much higher level than those found in most IT-based faculties in Nigerian universities and polytechnics. Customers tend to believe that any problem that cannot be solved in the cluster can probably not be solved anywhere else in the country. This accounts for the wide patronage of the cluster by customers across the nation.

Lessons Learned and Policy Implications

The most important lessons from the experience of the Otigba computer cluster center on *policy and institutional barriers against small firms,* which have constrained the progress of industrial growth in a country generally known for the entrepreneurship of its citizens. Three sets of systemic institutional biases work against small businesses in the Otigba cluster. First, government policy has long favored large, state-owned enterprises, in which the government has invested considerable efforts and resources with little return. Although there have been small business initiatives as well, the efforts have not translated into real service support to SMEs. Second, while the Nigerian government has formulated industrial and sectoral policies, there has been no explicit mechanism for differentiating across size and product groups. For instance, Nigeria now has an ICT policy, it is not specific about its intended effects on product groups or about how it will foster their growth. Support from the state has, up until now, been reactive, with no initiatives to facilitate firm entry. This is the reason for the pervasively small size of enterprises, which tend to struggle to find starting capital.

The *role of collective action,* which should be promoted by governments, has been a major source of support to the Otigba Computer Village cluster. There are several IT-based associations in the country, including the Computer Association of Nigeria, Institute of Software Practitioners of Nigeria, Internet Service Providers Association of Nigeria, and Association of Telecommunications Companies of Nigeria. A number of events led to the formation of the Nigerian Computer Society (NCS) as an all-embracing IT body for Nigeria. All types of IT professionals—both individual and corporate—are registered with NCS while operating in their various interest groups. Some members of CAPDAN in the Otigba cluster are registered with NCS. The NCS has been using its political leverage to pursue diverse issues of relevance to IT development in the country. Specifically, it has succeeded in lobbying for further reductions in duties on certain categories of computer components and accessories. Since 2002, this has resulted in further reductions in tariffs.

References

Abiola, Boladale O. 2006. "Knowledge, Technology and Growth: The Case Study of Otigba Computer Village Cluster in Nigeria." Unpublished paper, Knowledge for Development Program, World Bank, Washington, DC. April.

Bamiro, O. A., and A. J. Alos. 2003. "Industry Research on the Applications Software Sector in Nigeria." Lagos Business School, Pan-African University.

Kash, D. E., R. N. Auger, and N. Li. 2004. "An Exceptional Development Pattern." *Technological Forecasting and Social Change* 71(8): 777–797.

Mathews, John A. 2006. "Electronics in Taiwan—A Case of Technological Learning." In Vandana Chandra (ed.), *Technology, Adaptation, and Exports—How Some Developing Countries Got It Right.* Washington, DC: World Bank.

Oyelaran-Oyeyinka, Banji. 2005. "Learning in Local Systems and Global Links: The Otigba Computer Hardware Cluster in Nigeria." UNU-INTECH, Maastricht.

———. 2006. "Learning Hi-Tech and Knowledge in Local Systems: The Otigba Computer Hardware Cluster in Nigeria." Working Paper 2006-007, Institute for New Technologies, United Nations University, Maastricht. January.

7

Handicraft and Furniture Clusters in Tanzania

Flora Musonda with Catherine Nyaki Adeya and Boladale Oluyomi Abiola

Micro and small enterprises (MSEs) are dominant actors in the economies of many developing countries, and even more so of the least developed countries, such as Tanzania. These enterprises accommodate a workforce largely characterized by low levels of education and skill. Major challenges include low productivity, lack of capital accumulation, and labor-intensive (though capital-saving) production.

Although the Tanzanian government has tried different economic development models since the country's independence in 1961, it only recently recognized the potential socioeconomic contribution of MSEs. This policy change was justified by studies that estimate that one-third of Tanzania's GDP originates from the informal sector, and particularly from MSEs. According to the Informal Sector Survey of 1991, there were 1.7 million businesses operating in the informal sector and employing about 3 million people, or 20 percent of the Tanzanian workforce.

Because the informal sector was long neglected, there are systemic and institutional issues that tend to define the sector's trajectory. They include the heavy costs of compliance with government regulations and taxation standards, inadequate working premises, limited access to finance, lack of entrepreneurship skills, lack of marketing expertise and business training, low technology levels, and lack of information. There are also weaknesses in the institutional structures that support the informal sector, such as business associations; these are for the most part weak, fragmented, and uncoordinated. The sector also lacks clear policy guidance from government authorities.

In spite of these challenges, MSEs have survived over time and at times have even produced relatively good-quality products despite intensified competition following import liberalization. What, then, has been the source of the relative success of MSEs?

We hypothesize that the survival of MSEs and their production of good-quality products lies in the nature of their organization, notably, clustering. In examining incidences of clustering, we selected two MSE clusters in Tanzania: the Mwenge handicrafts cluster and the Keko wood and furniture cluster.

Between the mid-1990s and early 2000, the real output of the two industries grew by 13.8 percent. The wood and furniture industries had the highest growth in real output: 29.8 percent. Real value added in selected manufacturing industries grew by 22.6 percent, with the wood and furniture industry having the highest value addition of 38 percent, followed by the textiles and garment industry, with an increase of 34 percent. While the subsector grew in real output and value addition, employment fell by 7 percent despite the high real growth.

This relatively remarkable record has its source in other dynamics within the economy, one of which is the migration of skills from large-scale enterprises to the so-called informal economy. It is important to understand this dynamic and to design appropriate policies to support the clusters that benefit from it, as well as to nurture their nascent entrepreneurship.

We used a survey questionnaire supplemented by case studies of selected enterprises to collect the data for this study. Two separate surveys were carried out—in 1997 and 2004. The survey questionnaire contained both open- and close-ended questions designed to capture basic firm and owner characteristics, production and marketing performance, technological capabilities, networking and interfirm links, and the views of the firm owners on the existence and development of the clusters. The sample for the survey was made up of 60 firms from the two clusters that were interviewed in 1997 and in 2004. A sample of 20 firms on average was selected from each of the two clusters. In 2004 the approach was to interview the same set of enterprises that was studied in 1997 except where specific firms could not be found. In most cases it was possible to interview the same firms, but some in the Keko cluster no longer existed or had left the cluster.

Cluster Profiles

The furniture and handicraft sectors in Tanzania comprise a predominant number of small-scale enterprises and a few large firms utilizing simple technologies; the workforces of both have relatively low skill levels compared with internationally competitive enterprises. Our study provided a summary of the clusters' main actors and sources of knowledge, product types, inputs, and technology:

Key actors. The clusters include a number of large enterprises amid a larger number of small and medium enterprises. Average firm size varies from 130 employees to as few as 2 in microenterprises.

Sources of knowledge. Handicraft and furniture firms rely largely on apprenticeship skills acquired through learning by doing. Owners are often reluctant to invest in training because of the fear that employees will leave and start their own businesses once they are well trained. At this level of economic activity, actors have few links with universities but rely considerably on customers and input suppliers for knowledge and information.

Input suppliers and product market. Input suppliers are mostly sawmills and timber and logging companies. Some have developed long-term ties with cluster enterprises, but the market is always in flux and there are always new entrants that offer competitive prices. The product market is made up of actors in the furniture construction industry, and mostly tourists in the handicraft component of the cluster. In what follows we provide a general profile of the interlocking clusters, distinguished by product specialization.

The Mwenge Handicrafts Cluster

The Mwenge handicrafts cluster is located in the Tanzanian capital, Dar-es-Salaam, in the Kinondoni district. It is estimated that the cluster had 2,200 members in 1995, the last year for which data are available. The cluster is well organized and has its own trade associations, with governance rules and elected officials. There are two registered groups, the Mwenge Arts and Crafts Dealers Association and *Chama cha Wachonga Sanaa na Wauzaji Tanzania*, which represents carvers.

The cluster has both formal and informal origins. (A cluster with a formal origin is a purposefully designed and promoted agglomeration of enterprises.) In the past, arts and carving activities were widespread along the main roads of Dar-es-Salaam and operated with little organization and coordination. Because the enterprises were not formally registered, city authorities subjected them to continuous harassment and, in the end, the craftsmen and women were evicted from their former locations and sent into the current area as a way of "keeping the city clean." The forced relocation resulted in considerable difficulties for the entrepreneurs, largely because they had been moved away from areas familiar to their customers. However, their new location gradually developed over time and has gained considerable popularity among carving and art businesses. The Mwenge cluster has expanded significantly and is currently located in a protected area recognized by the Dar-es-Salaam City Council. The intended future purpose of the area is to accommodate all handicrafts dealers, particularly in the carving business and its auxiliaries.

The cluster is relatively well organized, with well-kept shops and diverse displays of merchandise. The key actors are carvers and their apprentices, who perform both production and marketing functions and interact closely with the merchandise sellers who also run shops within the cluster. In order to establish a market niche, cluster carvers have tried unsuccessfully to gain status as the sole manufacturers and sellers of the renowned Makonde carvings, produced from African blackwood by the Makonde people of southern Tanzania. These carvings are purchased largely by tourists as souvenirs, gifts, or for further trading. The cluster has attracted the attention of multilateral organizations, among them the International Labour Organization. ILO and other UN agencies provide advice to associations and carry out studies that inform government policy, particularly on the employment implications of enterprise support.

Marketing activities are carried out on an individual basis, and each firm has its own plans and future prospects, with limited success in gaining footholds in outside markets such as South Africa and Europe. Because the cluster lacks collective market and export support, enterprises still find it difficult to compete outside Tanzania. However, the government has established a college for handicrafts at Bagamoyo in recognition of the commercial and cultural importance of this art form. It is expected that this initiative will promote the acquisition of higher skills, leading to better product quality in the cluster.

The Keko Furniture-Making Cluster

The Keko furniture cluster, located near Chang'ombe Road in Dar-es-Salaam, has its roots in the growth of five key firms: Matharu Wood Works, Pan African Enterprises, Palray Limited, Jaffery Industry Limited, and Kilimanjaro furniture. All five were established by entrepreneurs of Indian origin in the 1970s. The firms began with machinery and equipment for timber cutting and cleaning, and offered manufactured furniture for sale including chairs, beds, and tables. In the Keko cluster, timber and wood enterprises are usually found contiguous to one another.[1]

---

1. Wood products constitute 0.7 percent of Tanzania's total exports (amounting to US$4 million in 2000); however, this figure is nearly equal to Tanzania's imports of wood products (US$3.46 million in the same year). The Sao Hill plantation in the Mufindi district holds 50 percent of the 83,000 hectares owned by the government. Major species grown include pine, cypress, eucalyptus, and teak.

Box 7.1. *Agglomerative benefits in the furniture and handicraft clusters*

Tamwood Crafts, Mwenge Express Furniture, and Eliza Timber Company are three small companies that produce wood products and furniture using apprentice-based skills. The enterprises' average number of employees is between 15 and 20 workers. Tamwood Crafts manufactures standard products such as sofas and armchairs. The firm produces on average of four furniture sets per month for large customers, such as hotels, as well as private customers. Tamwood Crafts uses woods such as cypress, hardwood, and pine purchased from the two other companies, Eliza Timber and Express Furniture. These companies are, in turn, linked with logging and timber firms. This arrangement, and the competition it generates, helps to increase input and product quality. These links show the potential benefits of being within the same geographic space and specializing in different segments of the same value chain. Trust and reliability develop over time, and transaction costs are reduced as a result of the localized learning and information sharing that benefit from proximity. Geographic location and specialization are the defining characteristics of an enterprise cluster.

In the same vicinity, a number of small individual timber sellers who also made furniture developed. In addition, there were individuals who made furniture of varying quality and whose production depended on the availability of cheap timber. Over time, increased demand forced an integration of this latter group of entrepreneurs into the activities of the large firms and the timber sellers. The integration also drew additional individuals from outside the cluster who had carpentry skills and were looking for employment (box 7.1).

Unlike the Mwenge cluster, the Keko furniture cluster is not formally protected, and the space it occupies is not provided by the government. The cluster has developed a reputation for producing a wide range of quality furniture at reasonable prices. Space limitations and a search for new markets have led some entrepreneurs to take their products to other parts of town such as Ilala, Namanga, Kinondoni, and Mwenge. At the same time, furniture makers from other areas are drawn to the Keko cluster because of its concentrated market and potential for collective efficiency gains.

Studying the cluster in 1997 and 2004, we observed a significant increase in the number of firms. In 1997 the cluster seemed more orderly; by 2004 some of the founding firms had left, but there had been a migration of a large number of new firms into the cluster.

Knowledge and Technology Aspects of the Mwenge and Keko Clusters

Education Levels

Entrepreneurs' education levels have a positive correlation to their performance. Education increases the possibility of knowledge-based production and innovation, and the ability to adapt to changes in the business environment. Table 7.1 shows the percentages of different educational levels among cluster firms.

A significant number of entrepreneurs dropped out of primary school (38.9 percent in Mwenge and 25 percent in Keko). However, in Mwenge, 22.2 percent had university degrees and advanced diplomas. Both clusters have a relatively high percentage of secondary school dropouts. If we compare across the clusters,

Table 7.1. *Education of entrepreneurs in the Mwenge and Keko Clusters (percent)*

Level of education	Mwenge	Keko
Primary school (seven years and below)	38.9	25.0
Secondary school and other postprimary schools (7–11 years)	22.2	50.0
Advanced secondary school, postsecondary diplomas (11–14 years)	16.7	25.0
University degree or advanced diploma (14 years and above)	22.2	0.0
Total	100.0	100.0

Source: Author's survey 2004.

we find that Keko has relatively more educated workers. The nature of furniture work demands innovation, so this tends to be reflected in the educational profile of workers. But it is unclear why the Keko cluster has such a sizeable number of educated individuals. Even more curious is the considerable percentage of university degrees or advanced diploma holders in the Mwenge cluster. One explanation of this phenomenon might be the migration of unemployed labor from the formal sector to self-employment. In the specific case of Keko, it could be that skill-based crafts such as furniture making, which is increasingly measured by quality, tend to attract educated workers as apprentices.

Firms indicated various sources of new ideas, designs, and innovation:

- Client specifications (45 percent)
- Catalogs and magazines (24 percent)
- Visiting trade fairs (15 percent)
- Hired designers (10 percent)
- Visiting trade fairs abroad (4 percent)
- Other (2 percent)

Clients are the most significant source of innovation and new designs in the cluster. This underlies the relative importance of buyers in influencing the rate and direction of change in both process and product. Eighty-five percent of the surveyed firms report that product quality has improved over time, while 2 percent believe it has "improved significantly." Compared with the first survey conducted in 1997, by 2004 enterprises seem to have acquired considerable marketing capability and show a positive response to the advent of new technologies. Many firms now produce catalogs of their products showing mobile phone contacts and e-mail addresses. This development is significant in improving marketing capabilities.

Knowledge and Information from Input Suppliers

Most firms in the Mwenge cluster sample procure inputs by subcontracting (74 percent). Others procure inputs from other MSEs (8 percent), through joint activities with other firms (10 percent), and by other means (8 percent). Among the Keko furniture traders, 75 percent of firms procure inputs by subcontracting and 25 percent procure them from other MSEs or through joint activities and other means. Many of these activities have fostered short- and long-term trade and production links within and outside the clusters, as well as reliance on several established producers.

Technology and Innovation Sources

Firms in the two clusters rely more on manual tools than on machinery in their production processes. The sharing of work tools among cluster firms is very common. There is also a frequent sharing of information, especially regarding the appropriate equipment and machinery to be purchased within the cluster. The 2004 survey shows that 70 percent of firms exchange information about sources and quality of technology. Only 5 percent of the surveyed firms reported that they get such information from government bodies or organizations.

Most innovations in the cluster are in two major areas of production: the use of different types of raw materials bought at competitive prices to make better-quality products, and product modifications. Modifications are made to produce newer or more modern designs to match changing consumer tastes and preferences. The absence of significant innovative activity in other areas can be attributed to the small size of most of the firms in each cluster. Small firm size and lack of adequate access to finance have a direct impact on firms' ability to finance research and development. Another important factor is the generally low skill levels found in the majority of firms surveyed.

The special skills considered in the survey include the skills needed to handle sophisticated equipment. Overall, the number of employees with technical skills was impressive, although such employees were not equally represented across firms. The greatest skill source is apprenticeship: 80 percent of employees obtained their skills from within the firm (on-the-job training). The remaining 20 percent obtained skills elsewhere, such as through previous employment, organized workshops, and vocational training. In-house training remains a major way for small enterprises to raise their skill base. Over 90 percent of the surveyed firms confirmed that apprenticeship was the most significant training opportunity for cluster firms. The remaining 10 percent of firms were shown to have a combination of organized workshops and in-house training sessions. The average duration of apprenticeship ranged from three months to four years. However, this duration differed among firms. Very few firms reported sending their employees to formal training sessions.

Policy and Incentives

The role of policy in promoting clustering is well documented in the economic literature, as summarized in the forthcoming work of Oyelaran-Oyeyinka and McCormick. In the Tanzanian clusters, direct policy incentives have been limited, but the clusters have benefited from functional policies that provided indirect support to cluster enterprises. Enterprise support takes different forms and includes the provision of general services and support from informal associations.

The policy model of cluster promotion in Latin America stresses the need for differentiated policies suitable for different cluster types depending on variables such as firm size, national orientation, and whether the cluster contains small and microenterprises, mass-production by advanced firms, or multinational companies (Altenburg and Meyer-Stamer 1999; Oyelaran-Oyeyinka and McCormick forthcoming). In other words, what works in one context may not necessarily work in others. In addition, cluster policies often need to be in harmony with industrial and entrepreneurial policies.

The type of MSEs found in Tanzania require specific policies that are not necessarily present in traditional industrial policies because their size and unique needs do not always match those of the formal sector. Interventions need to focus more firmly on strengthening infrastructure and the socioeconomic milieu that underpins entrepreneurship. For more advanced clusters (Altenburg and Meyer-Stamer 1999), we identified five policy areas in which governments can focus:

- Promoting a business-friendly environment by establishing permanent private–public consultation mechanisms.
- Stimulating interfirm cooperation and pushing firms to accept the need to follow best practices through government-sponsored benchmarking workshops run by outside local consultants
- Helping to set up industry information and advisory services at the state or provincial level
- Fostering relationships with local training and educational institutions
- Encouraging domestic firms to upgrade their technological and R&D capabilities

In all five areas, efforts are, at best, at a rudimentary stage in Tanzania. The Small Industries Development Organization (SIDO), established in 1973, has been active in the promotion of SMEs and clusters; it formalized its program in an official document issued in 2003. SIDO is supporting a proposal to establish and promote the growth of industrial clusters. It has recognized the value of collective support by organizing quarterly zonal fairs and exhibitions throughout the country. SIDO ordinarily subsidizes the participation of SMEs by paying for trade visits to other countries in the region such as Uganda and Kenya. It collaborates closely with local government authorities in allocating industrial lands and premises and establishing common facilities at the district level. Its mandate is to provide technology and product support; assist efforts in technical, business, and entrepreneurship training; provide information and advisory services, credit and financial guarantee services, and support for youth enterprises; and promote the capacity building of business associations.

The government has ensured a reasonable level of infrastructure. Electricity is available throughout the two clusters, although not in each individual store. In the handicrafts village, more than 50 percent of enterprises are connected to the grid. Water is available through communal standpipes, and mobile telephones are widely used.

Informal and Professional Associations

While formal institutions are necessary for the formation and sustenance of clusters, informal institutions also play a significant role. Informal institutions may manifest as loosely defined associations that act as mechanisms through which firms share and address concerns.

Our survey results showed that almost all firms are involved in one or more cluster-based associations, which act as valuable sources of information. The more formal associations are often instrumental in offering technological advice. Influential associations include the Sao Hill Forest Industries Association; Tanzania Chamber of Commerce, Industry, and Agriculture, founded in 1988; the Contractors' Registration Board, founded in 1997; and the Contractors Association of Tanzania, established in 2002.

The surveys asked what motivates firms to join these associations. Sixty percent of respondents stated that access to relevant or useful information on marketing and government policy was their reason for joining. About 30 percent engage in association activities because of tribal or kinship links.

Key Success Factors

The two clusters have different histories. Mwenge was assisted by government policy, while Keko emerged as a result of initiatives taken by a group of individuals. However, government involvement has had a significant impact on the evolution of both clusters. Infrastructure vital to both includes electricity, water, and buildings. Mwenge has better facilities, particularly in the provision of buildings, than Keko.

However, we did not find significant differences in cluster performance. It seems that MSEs in both have benefited from clustering. Both clusters face the same broad set of constraints, and what tends to distinguish a firm in each is the level of its internal capability. MSEs in these clusters are, for the most part, competitively weak and operate largely in the domestic market.

Both clusters witnessed significant growth between 1997 and 2004. Many new firms entered the clusters, indicating that through their success the clusters continue to draw new entrants. Cluster products have also grown to cover a wider range and have improved over time.

Lessons Learned and Policy Implications

By examining two MSE clusters in Tanzania, our study probed whether informal clusters can play an important role in the industrial development of less developed countries. Tanzania has not been able to successfully develop its manufacturing sector, although several models have been attempted. The analysis suggests that the unique characteristics of MSE clusters, including their potential for collective efficiency gains, offer significant potential for industrial development in a country like Tanzania.

Most of the firms studied confirm that they benefit from belonging to a network of other enterprises and regard their present location as ideal. In the two clusters, inter-firm relationships and links were present among older firms as well as new entrants. These links manifest as subcontracting, collaboration, and mechanisms for information exchange and dissemination. What motivates firms to subcontract is their search to achieve lower production costs and higher-quality products. These firms tend to be limited by an underdeveloped environment, and, unlike relatively sophisticated clusters found in advanced economies, their products are limited to the domestic market, with no ability to compete outside their borders.

Authorities responsible for generating industrial development and sustained economic activity should consider policies to promote cluster development. Policy that supports clustering raises the possibility of success, particularly when combined with selective government intervention. The key to success in implementing such policies is the preexistence or establishment of enabling institutions. In Tanzania, the formal institutions created by the government to support the growth of MSEs have been inadequate and ineffective.

The government should provide further assistance through R&D initiatives that enhance the technological and production capabilities of MSEs with a focus on upgrading local products and skills. In addition, MSEs should have greater access to a wider variety of financing options. For example, in a cluster setting, financing could be arranged based on a collective collateral model in which repayment enforcement was based on a system similar to that of cooperatives. A number of successful microfinance systems are based on this institutional arrangement. Finally, improvements in infrastructure and utilities such as electricity, telecommunication, water services, and housing for business are imperative for sustained economic growth and the expansion of clusters.

Sources Consulted

Aerroe, Anders. 1992. "New Path Ways to Industrialization in Tanzania: Theoretical and Strategic Considerations." IDS Bulletin 23 (2): 15–20.

Altenburg, Tilman, and Jörg Meyer-Stamer. 1999. "How to Promote Clusters. Policy Experiences from Latin America." *World Development* 27 (9).

Amin, A., and R. Robins. 1990. "Industrial Districts and Regional Development: Limits and Possibilities." In F. Pyke, G. Becattini, and W. Sengenberger, eds., *Industrial District and Interfirm Cooperation in Italy.* Geneva: International Institute for Labor Studies.

Barr, A. 1998. "Enterprise Performance and the Functional Diversity of Social Capital." Oxford Centre for the Study of African Economies WPS/98-1.

Becattini, G. 1989. "Sectors and/or Districts: Some Remarks on the Conceptual Foundations of Industrial Economics." In E. Goodman and J. Bamford, eds., *Small Firms and Industrial Districts in Italy.* London: Routledge.

———. 1990. "The Marshallian Industrial District as a Socio-economic Notion." In F. Pyke, G. Becattini, and W. Sengenberger, eds., *Industrial District and Interfirm Cooperation in Italy.* Geneva: International Institute for Labor Studies.

Berry, A., E. Rodriguez, and H. Sandee. 2002. "Firm and Group Dynamics in the Small and Medium Enterprise Sector in Indonesia." *Small Business Economics* 18: 163–175.

ESRF. 1997. Micro and Small Enterprise (MSE) Framework in Tanzania. Dar-es-Salaam: ESRF.

Harding, A., M. Soderbon, and Teal Francis. 2002. Survival and Success among African Manufacturing Firms. CSAE, University of Oxford.

Humphrey, J. 1995. "Trust and the Transformation of Supplier Relations in Indian Industry." In C. Lane and R. Bachman, eds., Trust Within and Between Organizations. Oxford: Oxford University Press.

Humphrey, J. and Hubert Schmitz. 2002. "Developing Country Firms in the World Economy: Governance and Upgrading in Global Value Chains." Duisburg INEF Report 61/2002.

Liedholm, C., and D. C. Mead. 1999. *Small Enterprises and Economic Development, The Dynamics of Micro and Small Enterprises.* London, New York.

Liedholm, C. 2002. "Small Firm Dynamics: Evidence from Africa and Latin American." *Small Business Economics* 181: 227–242.

McCormick, D. 1999. "African Enterprise Clusters and Industrialization: Theory and Reality," *World Development* 27 (9): 1531–1551.

McCormick, D., and C. Rogerson, eds. 2003. *Clothing and Footwear in African Industrialisation.* Pretoria: Africa Institute of South Africa.

McCormick. D., P. Kimuyu, and M. Kinyanjui 2001. "Kenya's Garment Industry: An Institutional view of Medium and Large Firms." Working Paper 531, IDS, University of Nairobi.

Nadvi, K., and H. Schmitz. 1994. "Industrial Clusters in Less Developed Countries: Review of Experiences and Research Agenda." Brighton IDS Discussion Paper 339.

Oyelaran-Oyeyinka, B., and D. McCormick, eds. Forthcoming (May 2007). *Industrial Clusters and Innovation Systems in Africa: Learning Institutions and Competition.* Tokyo: United Nations University Press.

Pyke, F., and W. Sengenberger, eds. 1992. *Industrial Districts and Local Economic Regeneration.* Geneva: International Institute for Labor Studies.

Pyke, F. 1992. *Industrial Development through Small-Firm Cooperation: Theory and Practice.* Geneva: ILO.

Pyke, F., G. Becattini, and W. Sengenberger, eds. 1990. *Industrial Districts and Inter-firm Cooperation in Italy.* Geneva: International Institute for Labor Studies.

Schmitz, H. 1990. "Small Firms and Flexible Specialization in Developing Countries." *Labor and Society* 15 (3).

———. 1995. "Small Shoemakers and Fordist Giants: Tale of a Supercluster." *World Development* 23.

———. 1995. "Collective Efficiency: Growth Path for Small-scale Industry." *The Journal of Development Studies* 31 (4): 529–566.

———. 1999. "Collective Efficiency and Increasing Returns." *Cambridge Journal of Economics* 23 (4): 465–483.

Schmitz, H., and K. Nadvi. 1999. "Clustering and Industrialization: Introduction." World Development 27 (9) 1503–1514.

8

The Lake Victoria Fishing Cluster in Uganda

Rose Kiggundu

In 1997, the European Union (EU) applied to Ugandan fish exports a set of sanitary and phytosanitary (SPS) standards that led to a conditional ban on one of the country's most important exports.[1] When the country's fish processors and exporters were unable to meet the standards, the industry was plunged into a severe export crisis, as fish processors were locked out of their largest and most lucrative market for three long years. At the time, the country was still recovering from a troubled past and remained dependent on a few traditional agricultural exports, notably coffee, the global trading prices of which were falling sharply. Because processed fish were the most important of the country's nontraditional agricultural exports, swift and decisive action to induce the European Union to lift the ban was imperative. The industry had no choice but to become compliant with the EU standards.

The case of fish processing for export in Uganda provides an interesting example of how a cluster of technologically weak firms in Africa overcame a serious challenge through networking, linkages, learning, and upgrading. It remains to be seen whether that experience will enable the country to upgrade other sectors and surmount future challenges.

Although access to the EU market was regained after a period of process-related technological learning, Uganda has not yet succeeded in translating its response to the EU fish ban into a more cohesive and proactive program of innovation and technological capacity development that might provide a basis for sustained export competitiveness of the fish-processing and other sectors.

Profile and Organization of the Clusters

Schmitz (1992) defines a cluster as a geographic and sectoral agglomeration of enterprises—an area ranging in size from less than a square kilometer to a medium-size city or a small subregion of a country.[2]

---

1. This chapter was prepared by Rose Kiggundu, drawing on her chapter, "Learning to Change: Why the Fish Processing Clusters in Uganda Learned to Upgrade," in Oyelaran-Oyeyinka and McCormick (forthcoming).
2. Schmitz's definition, like Porter's (1990), contains both a geographic or spatial dimension and a sectoral dimension. But, as McCormick (2004: 1–2) argues, "the difficulties of transport and communication in Africa as well as the prevalence of fairly small clusters make Schmitz's approach better suited to the discussion of African clusters."

Table 8.1. *Geographical location of fish-processing plants by nearest city in Uganda, March 2004*

Number of plants in city	Plants located in same suburb within city	Suburb where plants are located	District
5 (Kampala)	Plant 1 Plant 2	Nakawa Industrial area	Kampala
	Plant 3	Old Kampala	Kampala
	Plant 4	Kanyanya	Kampala
	Plant 5	Luzira	Kampala
5 (Jinja)	Plant 6	Jinja	Jinja
	Plant 7	Jinja	Jinja
	Plant 8	Jinja	Jinja
	Plant 9	Jinja	Jinja
	Plant 10	Jinja	Jinja
3 (Entebbe)	Plant 11 Plant 12	Entebbe Municipality	Wakiso
	Plant 13	Kisubi	Wakiso
1 (Kalisizo)	Plant 14	Kalisizo	Rakai
1 (Kyotera)	Plant 15	Kasensero	Rakai
1 (Masaka)	Plant 16	Masaka	Masaka
1 (Busia)	Plant 17	Busia	Busia

Source: Kiggundu 2005.

Fish-processing and -exporting firms in Uganda are not all clustered in a particular geographical city or subregion but are found in several cities surrounding Lake Victoria (table 8.1). Of the 17 plants in the country, 10 are located near two major cities, Kampala and Jinja, the latter being about 80 kilometers east of Kampala. Thus it would be fair to speak of two clusters of five plants each in Jinja and Kampala. There are important locational differences between the Jinja cluster and Kampala cluster.

While the distances between plants in the Jinja cluster are very small, three of the five firms in the Kampala cluster are located in different suburbs or parts of the city, for a total cluster area of more than one square kilometer. The Kampala-Entebbe subregion, with three plants, and the Masaka-Kyotera subregions, with four, may also be considered agglomerations. Both of these subregions are located in a geographical area known as the central region. However, the idea of a central-region cluster may be inappropriate given the long distances and notable differences in the state of infrastructure, utilities, and general state of development in the two subregions. Masaka City, for instance, lies about 120 kilometers from Kampala, making it difficult for firms to benefit from economies of agglomeration.

Clustering is often associated in the literature (for example, Schmitz 1997 and McCormick 1999) with four key advantages for member firms—market access, labor-market pooling, intermediate input effects, and technological spillovers. Uganda's fish-processing industry depends primarily on Lake Victoria, a fresh water lake shared by Tanzania, Kenya, and Uganda. The lake is the source of fresh export products, but because fish are highly perishable, the ability of the firms to handle, prepare, and export products in a "cold chain" is critical. For most firms, access to supplies and infrastructure must thus have provided greater locational advantages than market access alone.

All fish-processing firms in Uganda have had to provide intensive training for their workers to create a pool of local skills in factory-based fish preparation. The establishment of that skill base has benefited both new and old firms in the clusters, both through labor mobility and through the diffusion of ideas often associated with the routine interaction of workers. However, the clusters are marked by an acute absence of workers highly skilled in the more sophisticated aspects of fish processing. Formal technical and vocational institutes in Uganda have not provided adequate numbers of graduates qualified in industrial food processing. For their personnel needs, therefore, firms have relied on in-house training, usually of persons with only a few years of formal schooling. For more complex tasks such as product development, some firms have obtained technical expertise from buyers and other experts outside Uganda, as such skills are unavailable locally (Kiggundu 2005).

An additional benefit of clusters is that they often induce the emergence of suppliers who benefit from dealing with a group of customers located near one other. Suppliers sometimes even receive support from their customers. Both phenomena have been observed in Uganda's fish-processing clusters, but those benefits have been undermined by the failure to resolve the problem of reliance on a natural resource that cannot be harvested limitlessly. Research–industry linkages in fish processing are scarce even where research institutes can be found near the clusters.

Overall, agglomeration of fish-processing firms in several locations has provided only limited advantages.

Knowledge and Technology in the Clusters

It might be surprising that a resource-based activity should be based on diverse knowledge inputs. Yet the industrial fish-processing sector depends on a wide range of knowledge that is critical to firms' ability to compete in markets. For example, firms faced with designing or restructuring their plant layout need engineering knowledge. They also need knowledge of food science, food technology, chemistry, biochemistry, and microbiology to deal conduct tests, introduce new products, and apply Hazard Analysis and Critical Control Point (HACCP) procedures. Environmental knowledge is vital for proper waste management and effluent treatment. Though not readily available, knowledge of fisheries stock assessment and research on the reproductive biology of commercial species would be useful in the search for value-added technologies.

Before the EU ban, knowledge, information, and technical support were ineffectively distributed in Uganda's fish-processing industry. Although tremendous improvements were made during and after the ban in access to process-related knowledge, recent interviews in Uganda (Kiggundu 2005) indicate that the clusters still suffer from a shortage of critical knowledge inputs, including technical skills in value-adding technologies and diversification of raw materials (fish farming).

With the help of buyers, the clusters have made some progress in product development but have not yet shifted from the preparation and export of whole and semi-processed fish products (portions, fillets) to further processed products such as crumbed fish products, perfectly portioned fillets and loins, and ready-to-eat fresh and frozen products differentiated by weight. The incentives and skills needed to develop SPS-compliant and affordable fishing and collection vessels are still lacking.

The fish-processing clusters have obtained knowledge from various sources, although policies tend to affect firms differentially. Larger fish-processing and -exporting firms have gained access to financial resources and thus have greater opportunities to invest in technological change. They are able to employ well-educated and trainable managers, making it easy to absorb new techniques and to train other workers in the correct implementation of HACCP procedures. Small firms, by contrast, have more difficulty because they lack the financial, technical, and human resources to initiate and sustain technical change.

Because they are dealing with specialized firms, all engaged in the same activity, local and international business-development agencies, including the United Nations Industrial Development Organization (UNIDO), have been able to provide cost-effective support services and keep service-delivery costs low while maintaining outreach.[3]

Their efforts have facilitated the diffusion of knowledge, skills, and resources to foster technological change.

Policy and Incentives

Uganda's national fisheries department, created in 1948, began to conceive a development strategy for the fisheries sector as early as 1990 (Frielink 1990). The long list of responsibilities the fisheries department had taken on by that time (Frielink 1990) indicates that the Ugandan government, like many other governments in Sub-Saharan Africa, perceived itself as the main driver of economic activity in the fisheries sector and elsewhere.

In the 1980s and early 1990s, the government operated several state enterprises and projects, including those engaged in the production of fish nets (Uganda Fishnet Manufacturers); trawling (the Sino-Ugandan Fisheries Joint Venture); processing and distribution (Uganda Fisheries Industries Limited, which operated distribution centers and a fleet of trucks); and fishing supplies (the Artisanal Fisheries Rehabilitation Project, funded by the European Union). Many of these state operations had run into management and financial trouble before being closed or privatized. The key point is that despite this long history of public investments in the fisheries, no attention was paid to the need to build and support local systems for learning and innovation.

Bilateral and multilateral aid to Uganda surged with the advent of the economic stabilization and reform program in 1987. By 1990, it was generally felt that the development of the fishing industry was a matter for the private sector. Inspired by the new climate of free markets and private sector–led development, donors started building a case for the creation and strengthening of the policy and support environment surrounding the fisheries and other sectors. In the fisheries, the necessary environment would encourage profitable and efficient private sector involvement while also meeting objectives related to conservation and local nutrition. Conse-

---

3. UNIDO has been involved in providing considerable support to clusters in developing countries. Other agencies include the International Development Research Centre (IDRC) in Ottawa.

quently, a new donor-led strategy for the development of the fisheries sector began to emerge in the early 1990s. The main idea was to limit government involvement to those activities that warranted public sector intervention. These would include sector-level planning and monitoring, resource evaluation and statistics, regulation and enforcement, adaptive research and extension, export promotion and quality control, education and training, and rural credit (Frielink 1990). The Artisanal Fisheries Rehabilitation Project recommended that the fisheries department be reorganized into four independent divisions—a statistics and planning division, a management and law enforcement division, a research and development division, and an extension and training division.

In hindsight, it appears that this effort to reorganize the fisheries department was an attempt to build a stronger support system within the sector. However, these early efforts to strengthen and improve policy coordination neglected the technological improvements required in the fisheries. That prevailing fish-handling and -processing technology remained inferior did not seem to concern donors or the government.

The prolonged economic and political problems in Uganda had encouraged illegal fishing practices and detrimental fishing gear, such as small-mesh gill nets and seine nets (Ogutu-Ohwayo 1999). But even after the country returned to the rule of law in 1987, the right fishing gear did not immediately become available. Law enforcement officers, mainly extension workers from the department of fisheries, lacked the surveillance capacity to deal effectively with the situation. Low levels of interaction to exchange information, legal weaknesses, and a lack of political will also contributed to poor enforcement.

Even when regulations were put in place, they often were inconsistent or inadequately enforced. Mesh-size requirements, for instance, varied from lake to lake. On lakes Edward and George, the requirement was five inches, whereas the national requirement called for a smaller limit of three inches (Frielink 1990). Nor had the Fish and Crocodile Act of 1964 been updated to meet changed conditions and requirements of the fishing sector (Dhatemwa 1999). While the failure to enforce laws was often attributed to the paucity of information on available fish stocks, reliable catch statistics, shortages of boats, and financial difficulties, Frielink observed that the inherent conflict in the roles of field officers—called upon simultaneously to collect statistics, enforce laws, and provide extension services—also played a role.

At the fisheries department, inspectors could not adequately perform their duties. They lacked guidelines and standard operating procedures for inspecting landed fish, and hygiene conditions at landing sites, as well as procedures for sampling and tracing. The situation worsened after the government introduced its decentralization policy. District fisheries officers were no longer accountable to the national department and were subsequently found not to be adhering to instructions relating to the hygienic handling of fish (author's interviews at UNIDO's Uganda Integrated Programme, 2001).

The eventual improvements in processing fish for export were driven not by forces within Uganda or by donors, but by external developments in the international trading environment—developments that culminated in the 1997 EU ban. As early as 1991, EU Council Directive 91/493/EEC had required the Ugandan government to appoint a "competent authority" to oversee and manage the inspection process across the fisheries sector. Testing laboratories were to be designated and approved by the European Union to ensure product quality and safety. Infrastructure at landing sites was to be upgraded to improve sanitary conditions. The government had to ensure better hygiene and handling of fish throughout the supply chain—by fishermen, fish collectors, and other transporters—in addition to a whole host of improvements at industrial fish-processing plants. More specifically, fish-processing plants would be certified compliant only if they fulfilled requirements related to plant layout, operations, application of HACCP, and inspection. The list of compulsory requirements was long, complex, and required major restructuring.

Almost six years after the passing of Directive 91/493/EEC, the EU authorities had not visited Uganda to monitor compliance. Uganda, in the meantime, had made little effort to comply with the directive. But in February 1997 Spain discovered salmonella bacteria in fish exports from Uganda, which induced both Spain and Italy to impose a bilateral ban on fish exports from Uganda. In April 1997, the European Union required that fresh and frozen exports of Nile perch exports from the three countries sharing Lake Victoria to be systematically checked for salmonella as they entered the EU market.

Just as Uganda was learning new ways of dealing with the changed export conditions, a cholera outbreak hit the country in December 1997. On December 23 the European Union banned imports of fresh fish from Uganda, Kenya, Tanzania, and Mozambique citing insufficient measures to control the outbreak of cholera (Nathan Associates 2000). To make matters worse, a November 1998 EU inspection mission gathered anecdotal evidence of the use of agricultural chemicals, including pesticides, to capture fish by poisoning them. In March 1999 the Ugandan authorities announced a unilateral export ban to last until the safety of fishery products could be guaranteed. A month later, the European Union suspended imports of fish products from Uganda, Kenya, and Tanzania.

The importance of fishing to Uganda's economy ensured a sense of urgency in government and among development agencies to regain access to European markets by complying with the EU-imposed SPS measures. Ugandan firms made substantial investments to upgrade their processes, often going well beyond what was compulsory. Some introduced computer-aided devices for critical procedures, such as tracking yield and storage temperature. Some introduced automated methods and mechanized equipment that opened up a further process of technological learning. All firms upgraded their in-house laboratory capabilities. Their working knowledge of HACCP procedures, plant layout, industrial fish preparation, and exporting improved at the same time. In other words, a great deal of process-related learning occurred across the clusters in the effort to overcome the EU ban. Following a review mission in early October 2000, the European Union lifted the ban, upgrading Uganda to "List I" and permitting it to resume exports of fishery products to the European Union.

Nevertheless, close examination reveals that product upgrades lagged beyond process upgrades for three reasons. First, although pressure to upgrade products was increasingly felt in the clusters, incentives for private investment in product upgrading were still weak. Second, product upgrading was supported by the state but less decisively than was process upgrading. Notably, the state played a more direct role in providing process-related leadership and coordination by developing local standards and, through its fisheries inspection service, engaging in regular monitoring. It also sustained pressure on the clusters to keep up with improved process-related standards. Third, only a few actors in Uganda came together to respond to the product-upgrade challenge. For example, the processors business association (UFPEA) played a lesser role in the product-upgrading effort than it did with process-related upgrading. This was probably because clusters perceived the introduction of product-upgrading more as a competitive strategy requiring firm-level investment solutions, with joint efforts undertaken only vertically, through the supply chain, rather than horizontally and multilaterally among competing firms.

Processors jointly sought and obtained critical external knowledge to upgrade their processes because they faced a common difficulty—a common lack of knowledge needed to make the improvements demanded by the European Union. In response to the product-upgrading challenge, the clusters still faced this common difficulty. However, the knowledge inputs required appeared to be better provided through vertical and bilateral linkages that would minimize free-riding and supplier disloyalty.

Key Success Factors behind the Improvements in Fish Processing

What factors explain the ability of Uganda's fish processing and exporting industry to learn and innovate?

Overall, the clustering of fish-processing firms in several locations provided only limited advantages, supporting the conclusions of other analysts who caution that a mere geographical clustering of firms does not necessarily predict the development of systems of learning and innovation (Mytelka 2003).

By contrast, joint efforts—by firms in the fishing clusters, by public and private actors supporting the clusters, and by buyers outside the clusters—were critical in enabling Uganda's fish-processing clusters to upgrade their processes. The Ugandan government, international development agencies, the fish processors' association and private firms worked swiftly and cooperatively to rescue the industry. Fish-processing firms jointly explored solutions through their association. New arrangements between processing firms and their suppliers were introduced. Buyers of Nile perch in Europe formed an association that brokered information between the fish processors in Uganda and the European Commission in Brussels. A few of these buyers supported their suppliers in Uganda, helping them to comply with the EU rules, while others did not. But the joint search for solutions extended well beyond producers (fish-processing firms), their suppliers, and buyers. University departments in Uganda and international development agencies combined efforts to develop and jointly deliver a new training course in fisheries and aquaculture. Government departments and other providers of technical assistance introduced new ways of delivering services to fish-processing firms. A joint effort by the Ugandan government, international development agencies, fish-processing firms, and boat builders upgraded fish-collection craft and fishing canoes.

Success in the introduction of innovative activity depends on the degree to which key subsystems of the support system combine with firm-level competencies to promote learning and innovation (Kiggundu 2005). We attribute the ability of the fish-processing and -exporting clusters to engage in process-related learning and innovation processes to the productive interplay of several of those subsystems, among them institutional and organizational changes in market institutions, knowledge distribution and coordination, and associated sector-based policies, as well as to institutional changes in the finance subsystem and several firm-level factors. The latter include firm size, orientation to institutionally augmented markets, access to technical assistance, the financial position of firms, and personnel education.

Although the Nile perch exporting industry always enjoyed the benefits associated with firm size, a range of financing possibilities, export orientation, and other favorable characteristics, it was the flows and interrelationships that emerged within the fisheries system that resulted in a better fit between the improved support system and the firm-level competencies necessary for learning and innovation.

Lessons Learned and Policy Implications

What can we learn from Uganda's inability, so far, to translate its successful response to the EU fish bans of 1997–2000 into a more cohesive and proactive medium- and long-term process of technological capability development and innovation?

The pilot projects initiated by UNIDO's Uganda Integrated Programme attempted to extract lessons from the fisheries sector for the benefit of other food subsectors. However, the good fit observed in the post-ban fisheries system has not been apparent in the pilot projects. This implies that proactive interventions seeking to upgrade the capabilities of a sector ought to take into account the need to create such a fit. In other words, it is important to build a "sector-based system" within which learning and change can occur in each of the subsystems and in a manner that enables the knowledge gained in each subsystem to reinforce the others.

A second lesson is related to the first. While technological improvements introduced in the fisheries sector were no doubt significant, they were insufficient to sustain competitiveness. If we assume that the fish-processing industry has four main areas of production—capture, delivery to processing plants, processing, and transport to market—any technological improvement must interact and provide linkage across all areas to be fully effective.

Third, the experience of the fisheries sectors in Uganda (and Kenya) suggest that public efforts have a vital and multifaceted role to play in enhancing technological improvement for greater competitiveness. This role includes enforcing regulations and standards of performance, funding research, facilitating innovation, and arranging the provision of technical assistance. In addition, the Ugandan case underlines the vital role of public efforts in providing leadership and coordination of systemic learning, institutional change, and continued interaction with the various players to ensure that combined efforts bring about the desired flows of knowledge. For greater competitiveness of the fisheries sector in Uganda, Kenya, and Tanzania, public efforts will have to play this multifaceted role (Kiggundu 2006).

Uganda must invest in SPS capacity and the associated knowledge infrastructure. The country needs to focus on technical change as an important driver of economic growth and development, which requires effective delegation of powers to a high-profile competent authority, perhaps a renewed and upgraded Uganda National Council of Science and Technology (UNCST). Through unambiguous policy and with the involvement of all relevant actors, the national competent authority on technological upgrading should provide leadership in organizing background research across carefully selected sectors; evolving standards and performance targets for technological change; and developing new reward systems and support and enforcement mechanisms—all with an appropriate budget. Technological upgrading solutions will have to take account of sector-specific requirements and conditions. In this context, the competent authority should encourage productive relationships across all relevant public and private agencies, such as the investment authority, banks, government ministries, universities, business associations, suppliers, buyers, and research and training institutes.

References

Dhatemwa, C. M. 1999. "Harmonization of the Roles and Regulations of the Fishery Industry in Uganda." Report by the United Nations Food and Agricultural Organization (FAO) and the Government of Uganda.

Frielink, A. B. 1990. "Fisheries Development in Uganda." Report prepared by EuroConsult for Artisanal Fisheries Rehabilitation Project, Ministry of Agriculture, Animal Industry, and Fisheries, Republic of Uganda.

Kiggundu, R. 2005. "Innovations Systems and Development: The Journey of a Beleaguered Nile Perch Fishery in Uganda." PhD dissertation, United Nations University and Institute for New Technologies/MERIT-University of Maastricht, The Netherlands.

———. 2006. "Technological Change in Uganda's Fishery Exports." In Vandana Chandra (ed.), *Technology, Adaptation, and Exports—How Some Developing Countries Got It Right* (301–334). Washington, DC: World Bank.

McCormick, D. 1999. "African Enterprise Clusters and Industrialization: Theory and Reality." *World Development* 27(9): 1531–1551.

McCormick, D. 2004. "Upgrading MSE Clusters: Theoretical Frameworks and Political Approaches for African Industrialization." Paper presented at the Regional Conference on Innovation Systems and Innovative Clusters in Africa, February 18–20, University of Dar-es-Salaam, Tanzania.

Mytelka, L. 2003. "The Dynamics of Catching Up—The Relevance of an Innovation System Approach in Africa." In M. Muchie, P. Gammeltoft, and B. A. Lundvall (eds.), *Putting Africa First, The Making of African Innovation Systems.* Aalborg, Denmark: Aalborg University Press.

Nathan Associates. 2000. "Restrictions on Uganda's Fish Exports to the European Union." Report prepared for the United States Agency for International Development and the Private Sector Foundation Trade Policy Capacity Building Project, Uganda.

Ogutu-Ohwayo, R. 1999. "The Impact of Nile Perch Harvesting on Fish and Fisheries in Uganda." In G. Bahiigwa and E. Muramira (eds.), *Capacity Building for Integrating Environmental Considerations in Development Planning and Decision-Making with Particular Reference to the Fishing Industry in Uganda* (27–47). Economic Policy Research Center, Kampala Uganda.

Oyelaran-Oyeyinka, Banji, and Dorothy McCormick. Forthcoming (May 2007). *Industrial Clusters and Innovation Systems in Africa: Institutions, Policy and Markets.* Tokyo: United Nations University Press.

Schmitz, H. 1992. "On the Clustering of Small Firms." *IDS Bulletin* 23(3): 64-69.

———. 1997. "Collective Efficiency and Increasing Returns," IDS Working Paper 50, Brighton: Institute of Development Studies, University of Sussex. Revised and published in 1999 in *Cambridge Journal of Economics* 23(4): 465–483.

9

The Textile and Clothing Sector in Mauritius

Rojit Sawkut

Over the last 25 years Mauritius has recorded impressive economic achievements that have improved the living standards of its citizens, modernized the nation, and provided a window into the developed world. With a gross national income (GNI) per capita of US$5,030 in 2004, Mauritius is now categorized as an upper-middle-income economy. Within a very short period of time, outward-oriented strategies have transformed this small island with low agricultural productivity into a significant exporter with a manufacturing-based economy. The two sectors that have boosted the manufacturing performance of the Mauritian economy are sugar milling and textiles and clothing. However, the textile sector is now at risk.

The textile and clothing sector appeared in the government's agenda for the first time in the 1960s, when James Meade conducted a study on the Mauritian economy to find a solution for diversifying its sugar-based, monocrop economy. Meade urged the establishment of labor-intensive industries lest Mauritius fall into the "Malthusian trap."

The clothing sector in Mauritius plays an important role in the economy in terms of employment, foreign exchange earnings, and share of the GDP. In 2003 around 65,000 people—more than 60 percent of the manufacturing labor force—were engaged in the manufacture of clothing. In 2002 the sector accounted for 22.4 percent of GDP. In 2001 apparel accounted for some 56 percent of Mauritius' total exports of goods, and some 82 percent of its total manufactured exports.

Profile and Organization of the Sector

The textile and clothing sector of the Mauritian economy passed through two phases before entering its present phase with the phase-out of the Multifibre Arrangement (MFA) in January 2005. The first of the earlier phases occurred in the 1970s with the establishment of an export processing zone (EPZ). It was during these years that the first textile and clothing firms started to open in Mauritius. However, the growth of firms and jobs in the sector quickly stagnated. The second started with a boom in the textile sector in 1983. During the 1980s and early 1990s, textile and clothing firms began mushrooming all over the island. Foreign investors were attracted to Mauritius because of its pool of educated, unemployed labor available at cheap rates, and the investment-conducive environment set up by the government. The number of firms in the textile and clothing sector rose from 74

Table 9.1. *Number of textile and clothing firms (2000–2005)*

	March 2000	March 2001	March 2002	March 2003	June 2004	June 2005
Textile	65	62	59	57	43	41
Apparel	355	341	328	313	222	219

Source: Mauritian Central Statistical Office.

Table 9.2. *Employment in the textile and clothing sector (2000–2005)*

		March 2000	March 2001	March 2002	March 2003	June 2004	June 2005
Textile	Male					2,785	2,836
	Female					1,564	1,429
	Total	9,210	8,180	7,995	7,784	4,349	4,265
Apparel	Male					17,932	18,049
	Female					37,100	33,676
	Total	72,810	75,766	69,982	68,344	55,032	51,725

Source: Mauritian Central Statistical Office.

in 1983 to 435 in 1988. However, in the 1990s, the labor market became saturated, and wage rates in the textile and clothing sector began to increase; labor had to be imported to increase production. Firms started complaining that high wage rates were rendering their exports uncompetitive.

The first textile and clothing cluster in Mauritius was formed on October 7, 2002, with the regrouping of 17 firms. This cluster was formed after a year of research and discussions among different parties and stakeholders, following the initiatives of the National Productivity and Competitiveness Council (NPCC) and in collaboration with various institutions at the national and private sector levels.[1] This cluster is too young to permit conclusions about its degree of success, although it is still functioning.

After January 2005, the Mauritian textile and clothing sector entered a new phase—a third one—owing to changing global trading conditions in the textile sector. Since the phaseout of the MFA firms must be even more competitive if they wish to trade at the international level. In fact, though, the effects of the phaseout were felt even before January 2005 because some importers shifted their imports toward lower-cost producers before the phaseout to take full advantage of it. The value of Mauritian garment exports decreased by around 10 percent between 2002 and 2003. Table 9.1 shows the decrease in the number of firms in the textile and

---

1. A productivity implementation committee was set up in 2001 by the following public and private institutions: Ministry of Industry, Commerce, and International Trade; Ministry of Training, Skills Development and Productivity; Board of Investment; Export Processing Zone Development Authority; Industrial and Vocational Training Board; Joint Economic Council; Mauritius Chamber of Agriculture; Mauritius Chamber of Commerce and Industry; Mauritius Research Council; Mauritius Industrial Development Authority; National Productivity and Competitiveness Council; and Small and Medium Industries Development Organisation.

clothing sector in Mauritius during the period March 2000 through June 2005, while table 9.2 shows the evolution of employment levels over the same period.

As can be seen from the tables, both the number of firms and the number of employees decreased over the reported period, with the number of firms falling from 420 to 260, and the number of employees falling from 82,020 to 55,990. More firms are in the process of closing down, which means more job losses in the near future.

Although the bulk of activities in the textile and clothing sector of Mauritius are geared toward the manufacture of ready-made garments (94 percent of total textile and clothing exports in 2004), the importance, though minimal, of spinning and weaving firms in the local market should not be left out. In 2004 there were four firms in spinning and three in weaving (one did both). These figures should be compared with the 224 firms in the ready-made garment sector. The product base of ready-made garments is fairly narrow: four main products accounted for 91 percent of clothing exported in 2004: T-shirts (43 percent), pullovers (19 percent), shirts (12 percent), and trousers (18 percent). Most Mauritian shirts were destined for upscale markets; most t-shirts for low-end markets; and pullovers and trousers for mid-range markets (table 9.3). In 2004, as in all years since the beginning of the 1990s, most Mauritian clothing exports were geared toward three markets, which account for more than 80 percent of total clothing exports. The three markets and their respective shares in 2004 were the United States (29.3 percent); the United Kingdom (28.4 percent); and France (24.1 percent).

The more products that fall into the intermediate and basic categories, the higher the competition Mauritius has to face from cheap-labor-producing countries. Apart from shirts, most of the country's products are made for intermediate or low-end markets. One of the strategic approaches to surviving in the apparel market is to move up-market into high-end, high-value-added products where price competition is less severe and products fall into the "short supply" category.

Lall and Wignaraja (1998), studying the export competitiveness of the Mauritian economy, found Mauritius to be exceptionally vulnerable because of its heavy dependence on a few products, and because more than 80 percent of its manufactured exports come from one product group: clothing. They argued that once clothing exporters' wage-cost advantage was exhausted, export growth would depend on the ability to add value through backward integration (into textiles) and, within clothing, to upgrade quality and flexibility. To upgrade garment quality, investment is required not only in equipment, but also in organizational and labor skills, quality management, design, marketing, and response capabilities.

Table 9.3. *Quality component of different product lines, 2004*
Percent

Apparel	Knitwear (pullovers)	Light knits (T-shirts)	Bottoms (trousers)	Shirts
Up-market	20	20	20	65
Intermediate	80	20	80	35
Basic	0	60	0	0

Source: Joint Economic Council/Mauritius Export Processing Zone Association.

Jhamna (2000) conducted a survey in a study of the clothing sector of Mauritius. He ranked the problems that Mauritius-based garment manufacturers face as follows, in descending order of seriousness.

- Rise in wages
- Limited pool of labor
- Potential loss of markets
- Difficulty in adapting to technological change
- Low productivity

In his analysis Jhamna was also concerned with the relocation policy of firms. He ranked the reasons stated for firm relocation by his interviewees, again in descending order of seriousness:

- Low wages
- Investment incentives
- Government support
- Good infrastructure
- Political stability
- Skilled workers

The problem of high wages in Mauritius, which caused some firms to relocate to countries such as Madagascar and Mozambique, has abated somewhat since the time of Jhamna's study. In 2002 firms had to cope with a limited pool of available skilled labor, but today there is a pool of around 20,000 workers who were laid off from the textile and clothing sector and are looking for jobs. A lack of investment incentives and government support may now be the main factor causing firms to think about relocating.

Muradzikwa (2001) studied the southern African regional clothing and textile industry. He compared Mauritius, Malawi, and Zimbabwe in his study, and presented the hourly labor cost differences in 1997 among a number of countries (table 9.4). In terms of labor costs alone, Zimbabwe appears to have advantage over its counterparts both in the SADC region and among other non-SADC regions.

Knowledge and Technology Aspects of the Industry

A report prepared by the Ministry of Manpower Resources and Vocational and Technical Training in 1994 emphasized the importance of technical know-how and highlighted the low education levels of workers in the textile and clothing sector, who for the most part had come from the sugar industry. The report's main recommendation was to shift policy in the textile and clothing sector toward less labor-intensive, more high-tech production methods—methods that would succeed only if the labor force could adjust. The report focused on the need to upgrade some skills and learn others.

A survey prepared for the Industrial and Vocational Training Board in 1997 identified shortcomings in skills and training and recommended more active participation by the board in developing the sector's human resources (CITA 1997). It also suggested what the board should do to improve labor productivity. The board now coordinates a network of vocational training institutes and cooperates with major international institutes to ensure training in the most modern and sophisticated technologies. It also offers a higher national diploma in fashion and design.

Table 9.4. Hourly costs of unskilled labor in the textile industry, 1997

Region	Country	Unskilled labor cost (US$ per hour)
Organisation for Economic Co-operation and Development (OECD)	Germany	25.00
	UK	13.00
	U.S.A.	14.00
Non-OECD Europe	Hungary	2.40
	Turkey	2.00
Asia	China	0.55
	India	0.65
Southern African Development Community (SADC)	Malawi	0.52
	Mauritius	0.95
	South Africa	2.35
	Zambia	0.95
	Zimbabwe	0.50

Source: Adapted from Muradzikwa 2001.

A number of other institutions offer courses related to the textile and clothing industries. For instance:

- The Clothing Technology Centre, the technical arm of the Export Processing Zone Development Authority (EPZDA), hires qualified experts in textile and clothing from Mauritius and abroad to teach a variety of courses year round, including industrial pattern making, circular knitting, optimal sewing methods, screen printing, and line management.
- The textile technology department of the University of Mauritius also offers B.Sc. degrees in textile technology and textile fashion and design.
- The Manchester Metropolitan University in the United Kingdom offers a higher national diploma and B.Sc. in clothing production management in collaboration with Professor Basdeo Bissoondoyal College.
- At least five training institutions are registered with the Industrial and Vocational Training Board to meet training needs in textiles and clothing, while postsecondary programs cater to middle-management positions in the design and production of textiles and clothing.

The NPCC analyzed the textile and clothing sector of Mauritius in October 2003. The objective of the study was to formulate a corporate diagnosis of individual companies, using performance benchmarks to identify their strengths and weaknesses in areas such as management, organization, production, finance, and marketing. It used the Ramsey Productivity Models (RAPMODS), a tool for measuring the contribution of each unit of input to final output.

The assessment of the productivity indicators and the meetings with enterprises confirmed that the majority of enterprises in the textile and clothing sector were performing poorly (to varying degrees) in key areas—among them material utilization and procurement, productivity planning and budgeting, human resource management, financial management, inventory management, technology enhancement, international marketing, and competitive pricing.

Further discussions with enterprises revealed a number of issues affecting enterprise reactivity and performance, namely availability of collateral for loans; high interest on loans, overdrafts, and penalty costs; and excessive delays in bank loan processing.

Some enterprises have developed innovative approaches to addressing the constraints confronting them. Seven companies are pooling to reduce freight costs. Other enterprises are reducing interest on loans by borrowing in foreign exchange, implementing lean manufacturing or restructuring to improve enterprise productivity, improving lead times through restructuring (thus reducing both unnecessary delays and reliance on expensive air freight), and sharing orders with other enterprises to compensate for capacity deficits.

Similar positive experiences and the opportunities they represent have to be shared, multiplied, and supported throughout the industry. They represent opportunities for improvement that can be tapped with little or no significant monetary investment on the part of enterprises.

The main indicators for the industry show that, on average, small and medium enterprises (SMEs) have been investing more than larger firms, as shown by the average fixed assets which increased in the smaller sample. SMEs have also been slightly more productive, exhibiting higher capital productivity overall.

The total productivity measure for the industry in 2002 was 0.9706, a decline from 1.0119 in 2001.[2] The decline occurred because input costs rose faster than output. The measure suggests that the clothing industry, in aggregate, is not productive. However, a breakdown of the indicators reveals that performance is uneven from one enterprise to another, from one product group to another, and from one size of firm to another. The industry is not homogeneous, and this makes it risky to prescribe across-the-board solutions.

Policy and Incentives

The textile and clothing sector has enjoyed incentives from the Mauritian government since the beginning of 1980s. We will concentrate here on recent incentives. Most have been aimed at increasing the competitiveness of all manufacturing firms, including those in textiles and clothing. Very few policies have been geared only toward the textiles and clothing sector.

Before analyzing these policies, we should first mention the creation of Enterprise Mauritius (http://www.enterprisemauritius.biz). Incorporated as a public company on October 22, 2004, Enterprise Mauritius has as its primary purpose to provide seamless and responsive services to Mauritian enterprises within an integrated framework, with a view to enhancing their capability and competitive-

---

2. The total productivity measure (TPM) shows the amount of output generated by each rupee spent. If the TPM is less than 1, it means losses are being felt, and the enterprise is not effectively using its various inputs and factors of production. To produce an output the enterprise has to buy inputs from outside (these are represented as MI in the model), which are then converted to yield the final product. Thus, there are expenses related to conversion (CSI). The formula for obtaining the total productivity is as follows:

TPM = RSO/TSI

Where TSI = MI + CSI

ness. The founding board developed the organization's core strategy, defining its objectives:

- To monitor technology and serve as a focal point for technology diffusion
- To provide market information, develop competitive intelligence, and cater to export promotion
- To identify, track, and coordinate skill needs and trends
- To facilitate strategic partnerships and networking
- To provide advisory and consultancy services related to enterprise development
- To carry out other activities conducive to the attainment of the above objectives

Recent initiatives of Enterprise Mauritius are detailed below.

Small and Medium Enterprise Scheme. This scheme aims to promote the development of SMEs and integrate them into the industrial landscape. It applies to enterprises whose production equipment does not exceed 10 million Mauritian rupees in value. Under this scheme, the incentives given to the manufacturing firms are:

- No customs duty on production equipment
- 15 percent corporate tax
- Concessionary loan schemes to facilitate access to finance
- SME industrial estates equipped with IT facilities

Export Enterprise Scheme. The export enterprise certificate is granted to export-oriented enterprises that export their entire production. Authorization to sell a small percentage on the local market (10 to 20 percent) may be obtained, depending on the nature of the industrial activity. Under this scheme, the incentives given to the firms are:

- Duty-free import of raw materials and equipment
- 15 percent corporate tax
- Tax-free dividends
- No capital gains tax
- Free repatriation of profits, dividends, and capital
- 60 percent remission of custom duties on small buses used to transport workers
- Concessionary registration fees on purchases of land and buildings by new industrial enterprises

Strategic Local Enterprise Scheme. This scheme is intended for local manufacturing enterprises, which contribute to the economic, industrial, and technological development of the country. The incentives given to the firms are:

- 15 percent corporate tax
- No tax on dividends

Modernization and Expansion Scheme. The objective of this scheme is to accelerate the modernization, expansion, and diversification of existing manufacturing enterprises by encouraging them to invest in modern equipment, computerized production processes, and pollution control technology. The incentives given to firms are:

- No customs duty on production equipment.
- An income tax credit of 10 percent (over three years) on investments in new plants and machinery, provided that at least 10 million Mauritian rupees

are spent within two years of the date of certificate issue. This is in addition to existing capital allowances, which amount to 125 percent of capital expenditures.

- An additional allowance of 30 percent over the normal initial allowance of 50 percent on investments made in antipollution machinery or plants.

Roles and Activities of Industrial and Commercial Institutions

The Mauritius Industrial Export Development Authority (MIDA) is responsible for export promotion and the construction of industrial buildings. It also provides market intelligence through the Trade Information Centre, helps to organize the Mauritius international clothing and textile exhibition, and has several overseas offices to promote exports from Mauritius.

A new wing at the Investment Board—the Investment Promotion Department—helps potential investors and existing industrialists identify investment opportunities and joint-venture partners, locate land and factory buildings, and obtain clearances required prior to start-up.

The Mauritius Chamber of Commerce and Industry (http://www.mcci.org) is the leading private sector organization involved in the promotion of trade, industry, and tourism. It also represents the private sector before the government and other bodies. The chamber provides services related chiefly to customs, import, and export procedures and is an efficient provider of information about import and export markets.

The Mauritius Export Processing Zone Association (MEPZA, http://www.mepza.org), another private sector institution, sustains, promotes, and develops export activities and quality awareness; organizes workshops; and runs training programs for its members. The association has about 130 members operating mostly in the EPZ.

The mission of the Export Processing Zones Development Authority (EPZDA) is to help firms reach international standards of competitiveness through technical assistance, training, documentation, consultations, and other services. As such, its objective is to enable the export-oriented sectors of the economy to acquire the skills—both technical and managerial—needed for the successful transition of the country from a labor-abundant to a skill-abundant nation.

The Small and Medium Industries Development Organisation (SMIDO, http://www.intnet.mu/smido/) has been set up to help the development of SMEs. It acts as a facilitator and advisor in all sectors, including textiles and clothing, and provides various schemes and grants to help modernize SMEs.

Key Success Factors

The success of Mauritius's textile and clothing industry is based on the country's favorable environment for investment and the existence of preferential trading arrangements, addition to several exogenous factors.

Environment Conducive to Investment. Since the 1970s, the government has implemented policies that promote an environment conducive to investment, allowing the private sector to propel the economy. Export promotion began with the enactment of the Export Processing Zone Act in 1970. The EPZ was launched in 1971. The act provided incentives and concessions to enterprises exporting their products, including 10-year tax holidays.

As part of the process of liberalizing the economy, the government successfully implemented five successive stand-by arrangements and two structural adjustment programs between 1980 and 1986, which put in place the preconditions of sustainable, export-led growth.

In 1983, the government established the Mauritius Export Development and Investment Authority (MEDIA, now MIDA) to undertake investment missions and export promotions to boost the number of foreign investors and the total value of exports.

Devaluations of the rupee created a realistic exchange rate and helped make exports internationally competitive. The rupee was devalued by 30 percent in 1979 and by a further 20 percent in 1981.

During the 1980s, Mauritius had a pool of semi-educated labor that was available at a cheap rate. Although the majority of available laborers were unskilled, they were very versatile and adapted themselves easily to working conditions in the textile sector. Investors, mainly from abroad, took advantage of this ready labor force by setting up textile and clothing firms.

Preferential Trading Arrangements. Favorable trading terms, combined with ready access to markets in developed countries, induced foreign investors to set up textile and garment firms in Mauritius. Investors both domestic and foreign have successfully exploited the preferential access granted by the European Union and the United States under the Lomé Convention and the Generalized System of Preferences (GSP), respectively.

The first Lomé Convention, signed in 1975, was replaced by the Benin/Cotonou Convention in 2000 for a period of eight years. Under this preferential trade agreement, African, Caribbean, and Pacific states (ACP) enjoy duty-free and quota-free access to export their products to EU countries. The convention bestows considerable advantages. Non-ACP textile and garment exports are liable to a 17 percent duty on entry into the European Union.

The African Growth and Opportunity Act (AGOA), enacted in the United States on May 23, 2000, provided qualifying Sub-Saharan countries with duty-free access to the U.S. market for an eight-year period originally set to end in September 2008 but since extended to 2015. The act offers potentially vast benefits for African countries that can meet stringent rules of origin and other conditions.

Exogenous Factors. The success of the Mauritian textiles and clothing sector is partly attributable to factors beyond the control of the Mauritian government. Among the factors that have aided the growth of the Mauritian economy are the following:

- The products of low-cost exporting countries, especially Asian countries, fell under MFA restrictions during the 1980s. Thus Mauritius did not have to face tough competition in its exports to the United States, in particular. The third MFA, signed in 1982, constrained exports from several countries. It was in this context that investors from Hong Kong set up firms in Mauritius. Relocation enabled them to enjoy quota-free exports to the European Economic Community and to take advantage of unexploited quotas to the United States.
- The country's foreign exchange problem was eased due to a combination of falling oil prices and lower debt servicing arising from the depreciation of the overvalued U.S. dollar in 1984.

- During the same period, Taiwanese investors set up industries in Mauritius because of the appreciation of the Taiwanese dollar, which sapped Taiwan's competitiveness on the world market.
- After 1984, demand in European and American markets increased sharply, particularly with the appreciation of European currencies in relation to the Mauritian rupee, causing Mauritian goods to become more competitive.
- During the 1990s political uncertainty over the future of Hong Kong's reintegration into China encouraged investors to look for a safe haven; they relocated to Mauritius, bringing capital, marketing networks, and technological know-how.

Lessons Learned and Policy Implications

The conditions that led to the success of Mauritius's textiles and clothing sector have changed. Over the years, the government has had to provide more and more incentives to attract investment in this sector. Although these policies still appeal to the private sector, other factors, exogenous and endogenous, are no longer what they were.

With the phasing out of the MFA, in effect since January 2005, Mauritius must now compete with countries that formerly were restricted by quotas on their exports of textiles and clothing. In terms of market access, all of the world's countries have been on the same level playing field since January 2005. However, Mauritian exporters still benefit from the preferential tariff rates described above.

In the U.S. market, Mauritius continues to benefit under AGOA from duty-free entry of its clothing exports. This implies a tariff preference of around 17 to 18 percent, compared with the rates paid by some textile and wearing apparel exporters, such as those in China. Until AGOA expires, Mauritius's competitors in apparel exports to the United States are other countries that enjoy preferential tariff treatment under AGOA or another agreement. Those countries include Caribbean nations benefiting from the Caribbean Basin Trade and Partnership Act (also known as the Caribbean Basin Initiative), and Mexico under the North America Free Trade Agreement (NAFTA).

In the EU market, Mauritius will continue to enjoy duty-free access for its apparel exports under the Cotonou Agreement until 2008.[3] This implies a tariff margin of around 12 percent, the EU's most favored nation (MFN) tariff rate on clothing. But the European Union has so many preferential agreements that only 10 countries worldwide are subject to the full MFN treatment. Like Mauritius, other ACP countries are signatories to the Lomé/Cotonou Agreement, providing them duty-free access to the EU market. The EU's Everything But Arms (EBA) initiative provides tariff- and quota-free access to the EU market for almost all products from the world's least developed countries. (Mauritius does not fall in this category.) The 2004 enlargement of the European Union also affects Mauritius's apparel exports to Europe, because it brought several apparel producers into the free trade group. Thus a spectrum of countries already are competing with Mauritian garment exports in the EU market—on equally favorable terms.

---

3. The Cotonou Agreement maintains the MFA regime of trade between EU and ACP countries for a "preparatory period" of eight years (2000–2008), after which trade liberalization will be started for a transitional period of 12 years. For details of the Cotonou Agreement, see http://europa.eu.int/comm/development/body/cotonou/overview_en.htm.

Table 9.5. *Hourly labor cost across countries, 2002*
U.S. dollars

Madagascar	Bangladesh	S. Lanka	S. Africa	India	China	Mauritius
0.33	0.39	0.48	1.38	0.38	0.68–0.88	1.25

Source: Government of Mauritius and Mauritian Central Statistical Office.

After the phasing out of the Cotonou and AGOA preferences in 2008 and 2015, Mauritius will probably cease to benefit from the tariff preference margin in both the EU and U.S. markets. Like Mauritius, other countries currently benefiting from these two preferential agreements will suffer. But what is more challenging for Mauritius is that other countries currently benefiting from other preferential agreements (such as Mexico under NAFTA) will continue to benefit from preferences, and Mauritius will, therefore, have to become much more competitive.

The labor force in Mauritius is now more educated, skilled, and expensive. Hourly labor costs increased at an average of 5 percent per annum over the period 1990–2000, from $0.76 to $1.17, according to the country's Central Statistical Office. This has led to an erosion of competitiveness over time. Not only was there a sharp increase in the wage level during these years, but also a sharp increase relative to current levels in some Asian countries (table 9.5).

On the other hand, as wage rates have increased, so has labor productivity. But Mauritius's hourly labor cost is more than twice that of India and China, where productivity is higher. Tagg (2002) considered labor productivity in terms of pieces per operator per day and noted the following results: 18 in Mauritius, 18.2 in Taiwan, 19.8 in Thailand, and 20 in China.

Therefore the Mauritian apparel industry faces a very serious challenge: its productivity is lower than that of its competitors, whereas unit labor costs are higher. Although the unit labor cost is not the only cost factor, it is important because the production of apparel is highly labor intensive, and labor costs are a significant share of total production costs.

Mauritius' skilled labor force should be regarded as an asset that should be protected in the search for improved competitiveness. Because competing with giants like China and India in lower-end products is out of the question, Mauritius is working to position itself as a supplier of quality products, that is, as a niche producer in the fashion market and in other segments of the industry where the use of technology is intensive. Advanced, technology-based production, complemented by Mauritius' educated and skilled labor force, should open a window for the successful production and export of high-end products.

According to the Mauritius Export Processing Zone Association, the production of Mauritian textiles and clothing should reflect four principles: producing the right product, at the right price, at the right time, and under the right conditions. Producing the right products calls for training of the existing labor force and the development of quality awareness among both producers and employees. At the national level, the government recently initiated a training scheme for job seekers. Although the initiative was well conceived and implemented, some improvements are needed to better meet the current needs of the market. The training scheme should be more detailed at the micro level so that workers can be trained in each and every task involved in the production process. If necessary, Mauritius should import highly skilled labor to train its labor force.

As noted earlier, labor cost is not the only factor of production. Although labor costs in Mauritius are quite high compared with those of developing countries, they are low when compared to those of countries producing high-value products. Producing at the right price does not necessarily mean at the lowest price (with the lowest wages). Strategies should be developed to reduce lead time, use technologically advanced methods of production, and reduce the cost of holding large inventories. In Mauritius, many firms are revisiting their market strategies in the light of changing worldwide textile consumption patterns, aiming to upgrade their technology and enter higher-value-added market segments. They are modifying their production structures to achieve better integration and larger units so as to benefit from economies of scale and to meet more concentrated demand.

Chief among the initiatives that might help clothing firms restructure and adapt to current market needs are:

- Awareness campaigns and market information to help producers understand the opportunities open to them, such as exports under AGOA
- A continuous search for potential markets, potential clients, and competitive intelligence to help firms find new places and partners in the value chain
- Training facilities to retrain workers and improve their productivity
- Support for new schools of design that will supply creative designers and stylists as needed to help Mauritius's apparel industry aim higher in the market and create a niche market, perhaps for a Mauritian brand
- Support for training centers that will help firms find skilled workers when needed
- Affordable finance to help firms reorganize, modernize, and equip their plants with technologically advanced production techniques
- Support for studies of producers' needs and concerns, to underpin future action
- Continuous clustering and benchmarking exercises on a large scale.

References

CITA (Clothing Industry Training Authority). 1997. Final report on the training needs for the textile sector. Report prepared for the Industrial and Vocational Training Board

Jhamna, M. 2000. "Restructuring the Mauritian Clothing Industry in the Light of New Trade Agreements." University of Cape Town, August 2000.

Lall, S., and Wignaraja G. 1998. "Mauritius: Dynamising Export Competitiveness." Commonwealth Economic Paper 33, Commonwealth Secretariat, London.

Muradzikwa, S. 2001. "The Southern African Regional Clothing and Textile Industry: Case Studies of Malawi, Mauritius and Zimbabwe." DPRU, University of Cape Town, December 2001.

NPCC (National Productivity and Competitiveness Council). 2003. "Level 1 Assessment of Enterprise Performance." NPCC Final Report to the Textile Emergency Support Team. October 2.

Tagg, S. 2002. "Transaction Costs and Clothing and Textile Trade in SADC." DPRU Working Paper 02/64, University of Cape Town. April.

10

The Wine Cluster in South Africa

Eric Wood and David Kaplan

The South African wine industry grew significantly over the last decade, and it did so within a global market that has become extremely competitive with the entry of new players.[1] This phenomenal change to the industry was brought about by a combination of institutional, structural, and market-related factors. In 1992, South Africa accounted for 3 percent of the world's wine production and less than 0.3 percent of wine exports. That reflected the country's isolation during Apartheid. The lifting of sanctions on South Africa created a favorable environment for export growth. Exports grew from 20 to 177 million liters between 1992 and 2002, increasing as a proportion of the country's table wine production from 2.4 percent in 1992 to 32.3 percent in 2002. Over the same period, table wine production swelled from 426.6 to 567.2 million liters, or 33 percent. That growth was supported by new plantings and a shift away from growing grapes for distilling, but it was limited by a decrease in yields.

The volume of South African wine exports grew more rapidly over the decade 1992–2002 than those of other "New World" producers (table 10.1), albeit from a lower base. Australia and Chile had significantly larger absolute increases in export volumes.

Data were drawn from 24 interviews held with three industry institutions and 17 randomly chosen wine producers from different segments of the South African wine industry, conducted by Wood and Kaplan (2005) between April and June 2004. Each interview consisted of 2–3 hours and follow-up telephone calls. The focus of the interviews was on innovation within individual companies, the impact of innovation on performance, and the role of industry networks in supporting innovation within the industry. The 17 firms account for slightly less than 10 percent of South Africa's total wine sales.

This set of interviews built on a larger survey performed in 2003. That survey consisted of 41 interviews with 20 randomly chosen wine producers or wine companies, and 7 representatives of industry associations, research organizations, or other industry institutions. Together, the two surveys included 35 wine producers and companies, accounting for roughly 40 percent of South African wine sales in 2003. The results of the earlier survey are consistent with the more recent one.

---

1. Much of this study originally appeared in Wood and Kaplan 2005. It was adapted with the authors' permission by Catherine Nyaki Adeya and Boladale Oluyomi Abiola.

Table 10.1. *Export volumes of selected New World wine producers, 1992 and 2002*

	Australia	Chile	NZ	USA	RSA
1992 (m liters)	88	74	7*	147	20
2002 (m liters)	453	355	23	282	177
2002–1992 (m liters)	365	281	16	135	157
percent Δ 1992–2002	415	380	229	91	785

Source: Authors' survey
* Estimate.

Therefore, we are confident that the results from the sample of 17 most recent interviews can be regarded as indicative of the industry as a whole. This chapter is informed by data drawn from those interviews.

Organization of the Cluster

South Africa's wine producers can be divided into four segments, each with a different structure and focus. The four segments are the established producers, new producers, cooperative producers, and wholesalers (some of which produce wine, in addition to buying and selling it). Development in the different segments has been influenced by changes in the political and economic landscape of South Africa, as well as by changes in the industry.

Wine estates and none state wine farms are mostly small producers of quality wines. A wine estate is essentially a wine farm that grows grapes, makes wine, and bottles it on a single property. None state wine farms make wines in a cellar offsite or buy grapes from other growers. The number of small wine farms increased by more than 150 between 1999 and 2003. By 2003, South Africa had more than 80 wine estates and 260 nonestate wine farms.[2]

The increase in the number of small wineries is largely attributed to the ending of the quota system in the early 1990s, which is described later in the chapter. The demise of the quota system allowed startups to enter the industry for the first time in three decades and paved the way for some cooperative growers to make wine independently. The structure and capabilities of the new entrants differ from those of established producers. For this reason, we distinguish between new and established wine producers.[3] We will define established producers as wine estates and nonestate wine farms that were producing wine before 1994, and new producers as those established since the beginning of 1994.

South Africa's 66 cooperative producers are an important segment of the industry, owing to the large number of growers they represent. In 2003, they accounted for roughly two-thirds of the total grape crush. Historically, their primary focus

---

2. In the South African context, the term "certified wine" includes estate wine, wine of origin, or geographical unit wine, according to SAWIS (www.sawis.com). This accounts for virtually all table wine production as well as some wine of lesser quality.

3. A quota system, introduced in 1956, placed a statutory limit on the number of vines a farmer could grow. It allowed the Ko-operatieve Wijnbouwers Vereniging van Zuid Afrika Beperkt (KWV), formed in 1918, to set the size of the crop as well as control the location of the grapes. For 15 years, incoming vines were impounded.

Table 10.2. *Change in volume of production by industry segment, 1998–2003*
Cases of wine produced

	1998	2003	Percentage increase, 1998–2003
Producing wholesalers	250,000.0	1,250,000.0	400.0
New producers	1,630.2	13,021.4	698.7
Cooperatives	5,000.0	63,333.3	1166.7
Established producers	8,866.7	18,133.3	104.5
Total	33,573.2	168,930.4	403.2

Source: Wood and Kaplan 2005.

has been on basic wines sold in bulk. However, many cooperatives also produce some quality wine. In 2003, they accounted for more than 20 percent of production of certified wine. South Africa's top wine brands in international markets include some owned by cooperatives.

There are estimated to be 104 wholesalers operating in the South African wine industry. This group dominates wine sales, accounting for the sale of 62 percent of certified wine. The primary functions of the wholesalers in the supply chain are marketing, sales, and distribution. They buy and sell wine in bulk or bottled form. However 13 wholesalers, including some of the largest, also buy grapes and make their own wine. These are referred to in the industry as "producing wholesalers." From 1998 to 2003, the total cases of wine produced by the "producing wholesalers" increased by 400 percent (table 10.2). The remaining wholesalers are not involved in wine production.

Knowledge and Technology Aspects of the Cluster

The wine sector in South Africa has benefited from significant technical and marketing support from institutions. Technical support is provided through the partially state-funded science council for the agricultural industry, the Agricultural Research Council (ARC).[4] ARC Infruitec-Nietvoorbij was founded in 1997 through the merger of ARC–Stellenbosch Institute for Fruit Technology and ARC–Nietvoorbij Institute for Viticulture and Oenology. ARC Infruitec-Nietvoorbij is the largest of the ARC's 13 institutes. In addition to providing technical support, ARC Infruitec-Nietvoorbij also conducts research. The institute has 10 divisions, 7 of which are directly involved in wine research. These include soil science, disease management, pest management, postharvest (with an emphasis on yeasts), sustainable rural livelihoods, and technology management and transfer. Research is carried out at experimental farms in different areas, thus ensuring that different soils and climates are examined.

The key coordinating role in wine research is played by the Wine Industry Network for Expertise and Technology (Winetech). Winetech is the hub of an extensive network encompassing all aspects of the industry and scientists and technicians

---

4. The ARC is a statutory body established under the Agricultural Research Act. As one of the science councils in South Africa, its function is to promote agricultural research and the development and transfer of technology.

from the universities and ARC Infruitec-Nietvoorbij. Winetech serves as an advisory council to the South African Wine and Brandy Company (SAWB), a nonprofit company that represents wine producers, workers, and wholesalers. Winetech is governed by a board made up of five representatives of the various constituencies of the trade. Winetech allocates funding to research projects based on competitive bidding. Applicants for research funding submit proposals, which are channeled through four core committees: viticulture, training, technology transfer, and oenology. These committees weigh applications their program criteria. Programs include combating vine virus; optimal grape composition; *terroir* identification and utilization; and grapevine and wine biotechnology.

Winetech pays close attention to dissemination of research to end users. Whenever possible, Winetech-funded research projects must be presented to users and published in at least one academic and one popular magazine. Winetech publishes the *Journal of the South African Society for Oenology and Viticulture.* In addition, research is frequently published in a popular farmer's magazine. Winetech has a Web site and produces regular brochures. Finally, it organizes a large number of meetings within the industry as well as "road shows" to demonstrate new technological advances. The researchers themselves hold regular meetings with the industry and with specific industry individuals. Widespread use of viticulture and viniculture consultants means that an even larger proportion of producers are likely to be benefiting indirectly from Winetech research.

In 2000 SAWB assigned responsibility for the promotion of South African wines internationally to Wines of South Africa (WOSA). A private organization, WOSA acts on behalf of some 320 South African wine exporters. It is a fully independent, nonprofit entity recognized by the government as the export council for the wine industry. It is funded by a statutory levy on exports of bottled natural and sparkling wines, together with a major contribution from the South African Wine Industry Trust (SAWIT), established in 1999 to promote transformation and restructuring following deregulation of the industry and privatization of key cooperative institutions.

WOSA's mandate is to promote the export of South African wines in key international markets. It coordinates industry exhibits at major wine shows, effectively reducing the cost of trade show participation to individual industry players. It also increases the international visibility of local producers by bringing wine and lifestyle journalists to the Cape on an ongoing basis. In addition, WOSA holds the biannual Cape Wine trade exhibition, which draws more than 500 international trade visitors. WOSA works closely with the Western Cape Tourism Board to advance Cape wine tourism. Regular marketing seminars for executive decision makers in the WOSA membership bring international wine buyers and wholesalers to the country to discuss the market's changing needs, demands, and opportunities. Finally, WOSA has established importer committees in the United Kingdom, United States, and Canada. These importer committees include all leading exporters; their purpose is to help drive the strategy for South African wine in those markets.

More than 70 percent of the private respondents interviewed for this study said that they had used WOSA's services in some way, and all but one indicated that they viewed WOSA's contribution as important and beneficial. Another indicator of the effect WOSA has had in the industry is its impact on the strategic thinking of top managers who responded to our survey.

Several of the respondents recognized the significant influence that WOSA's activities have had on the perception of South African wines internationally. Producers expressed a strong interest in WOSA's brand concept and message and were clearly committed to playing an active and continuing role in formulating WOSA's strategy. The majority of producers expressed a significant degree of confidence in WOSA's leadership role in promoting South African wine, and particularly in its emphasis on wine quality and moving into higher-priced markets.

WOSA's reputation and capacities have been further enhanced by a unique international success it achieved in 2003. Forty-two million liters of EU wine imports from South Africa were exempted from import duty under the terms of the South African–European Union Free Trade Agreement. The benefit of the duty exemption went largely to supermarkets. Through the efforts of WOSA, U.K. supermarkets agreed to pool those resources and assigned control and coordination to WOSA for the further promotion of South African wine within the United Kingdom.

The indirect effects of WOSA's activities are at least as important as the direct services it offers. Of particular importance, WOSA's generic marketing initiative appears to have influenced the extent and nature of the relationship between individual players in the industry. Several respondents emphasized the limitations of their own marketing efforts and highlighted the importance to them of marketing successes among other local producers, particularly media coverage of leading South African wine producers. Historically, there had been relatively little coordination of international marketing efforts and little recognition of the interdependence of South African producers in building their brands.

Another industry body, the South African Wine Industry Information and Systems (SAWIS), provides important services that assist industry players in their marketing activities. It, too, is a not-for-profit company originally established to manage the industry's system for designating the origin of wines. SAWIS collects, processes, and disseminates detailed statistics on wine production and prices. It also makes available data on price movements in other wine producing countries. These statistics are widely referred to within the industry, serving as a critical guide in market negotiations and strategic planning.

Policy and Incentives

Two broad sets of policy initiatives, one related to the agricultural sector in general and another focused on the wine industry, were responsible for the significant success recorded in the wine clusters in recent years.

For more than 30 years until 1995 the South African wine sector was highly regulated. A quota system prescribed the total area that each producer could have under vines and set standard prices for grapes. Those prices were based on volume, irrespective of variety and quality. The system favored white wine production, which accounted for more than 80 percent of the wine produced at that time. The quota system was intended to address problems of surplus production in a constrained domestic market and to keep prices artificially high. It was administered centrally by the KWV (Koöperatieve Wijnbouwers Vereniging van Zuid-Afrika Bpkt). Founded in 1918 and a cooperative until 1997, KWV is now a group of private companies.

An important part of the quota system was the institution of cooperatives. With the exception of a few leading estates, all wine farmers were required to be members of the KWV. In addition, the majority of grape growers belonged to local cooperatives (of which there were nearly 70) and were required to sell all of their produce through their cooperatives. The quota system created incentives for grape growers to maximize grape yields per hectare, but this came at the expense of quality. Some producers, particularly those outside the cooperative system, chose to adopt good viticultural and wine-making practices to produce quality wine. But the bulk of grape and wine production was of poor quality. The cooperative system effectively maintained prices of poor-quality grapes at artificial levels and shielded the overwhelming majority of producers from consumer markets.

The ending of the quota system led to widespread changes in production. The changes included a shift toward varietals for which global demand was increasing. Thus, the share of red wine production more than doubled between 1995 and 2002, from 13 percent to 28 percent. New incentives were provided to promote extensive new planting and replanting. This initiative concentrated on noble, commercially important varieties—among them cabernet sauvignon, shiraz, merlot, sauvignon blanc, and chardonnay. The extent of this planting activity is illustrated by vineyard age. In 2002, 37 percent of the 110,000 vineyards were less than eight years old.

South Africa's wine-making regions are unique in their biodiversity. This means that they have the potential to produce a great variety of wines of distinctive character, reflecting the region in which the grapes were grown and the wine was made. With the repeal of the quota system, vineyard practices improved, as the focus shifted to improving grape quality, reducing vineyard yields, and maximizing the advantages of location.

Broad macroeconomic policies were the tools used to rid the country of the quota system, along with other old and discriminatory policies. The macroeconomic initiatives included:

- Liberalization of agricultural trade and deregulation of marketing agricultural products
- Implementation of land reform policies and programs
- Abolition of certain tax concessions and reduction of direct subsidies
- Introduction of a minimum wage for farmers.

The control board for individual agricultural sectors was abolished through legislation in 1996, and the National Agricultural Marketing Council took steps that helped to bring small-scale producers into the mainstream.

Key Success Factors

Key actors in the wine industry recognized that success depended on innovation at the technical and organizational levels. SAWB revealed the great premium it placed on innovation in its vision of building an industry that was "innovation-driven, market-directed and highly profitable, dominant in selected global market niches . . . (and reflecting) good citizenship and social responsibility." SAWB was formed to implement that vision—and to fill the void left by the KWV with the termination of the coordination function that KWV had provided to the industry. SAWB's structure mirrors its stated purpose, incorporating divisions focusing on basic and applied research, international market development, and social and political transformation. There is an explicit commitment to enhancing the competitiveness of the industry through innovation in every aspect of the industry. Within that broad vision, short-term goals have been identified. For example, WOSA has pursued SAWB's goal of expanding the volume of premium wines being exported for sale in high-end, international markets.

Increased attention to the marketing of South African wines has also contributed to the industry's international competitiveness. The competitive realities of the global market reinforced the institutional role of the SAWB, because global marketing of the country's brands is too big a job for individual firms. Membership in a network clearly provides an advantage.

Various forms of cooperation and collaboration among producers and other institutions in wine-producing regions play an important role in supporting innovation and help to overcome market imperfections and inefficiencies. Intense rivalry within the industry and competition at the firm level exist side by side with significant collaboration and cooperation. Firms competing fiercely for customers in the very limited local market also recognize the collective value of a strong South African brand and presence in export markets. Cooperation also helps to reduce the costs and risks associated with innovation, thereby increasing the profit potential and attractiveness to individual producers of engaging in innovation. The extent to which producers and institutions within an industry are able to cooperate thus influences the extent of innovation, and ultimately the level of international competitiveness.

Cooperative behavior among competing firms does not occur naturally; it is likely to require deliberate and sustained action. This applies particularly to the South African wine industry, which has only recently emerged from an extended period of external isolation, regulation, and major internal division (for example, between black workers and white owners, and between Afrikaans- and English-speaking owners).

Innovation altered not only marketing, but also wine-making processes and the choice of which wines to produce. The different segments of producers introduced entirely new wine products in years following the repeal of the quota system. Some producers consolidated their products, focusing on a small range of noble varieties and on particular market segments. Some producers were successful in increasing the quality of their wines through a major revision of viticultural practices. And some producers changed their strategy in marketing and branding their products.

Established producers engaged in extensive production innovation, largely in the area of viticulture. There were extensive replantings as well as new plantings. The planting initiative covered the majority of the vines of two producers in our sample. These and other firms obtained loans to fund the investment. For one, replanting was so extensive that production was halted for two years. Replanting appears to have been largely motivated by a growing appreciation of the local *terroir* and the need to improve grape quality by reconsidering the number of varieties grown and focusing on a limited number of noble varieties that were particularly suited to the soils and climates of the producers' vineyards. Changes in viniculture tended to be less dramatic, although one firm built a new cellar and put its viticulturalist in charge of winemaking.

Most of the established producers were actively engaged in exchanging production knowledge through collaboration. These included viticultural and vinicultural forums, a root-stock association, two varietal associations, the Winetech research network, and the Elsenburg training institute, which has vineyards and a cellar. Engagement with research initiatives, such as those falling under Winetech's umbrella, was limited to a minority of firms. The more successful firms tended to engage more effectively with Winetech. The most important source of knowledge, however, was private consultants used by all of these producers, but used most by the more successful firms.

We observed two distinct approaches to marketing among the established producers. One was characterized by an explicit focus on a limited number of geographical markets and clearly defined points of sale. All of the producers in this group had strong local market positions, built on well-known, long-established brands together with substantial direct consumer sales with relatively high profit margins. These direct sales, at the cellar door or in in-house restaurants, were an important means of building awareness of their wines, both among local and foreign consumers. Another way they generated interest in their brand was through restaurants, hotels, and other outlets where wine is sold for consumption on the premises. They also made sales through specialty wine shops, and one producer supplied to a high-end supermarket chain. Producers in this group are likely to have a single label, though one had two labels which were sold through different channels. There was strong emphasis on the importance of brand. Each producer articulated a clear, simple concept of what their brand represented and how it related to their products, assets, and history.

These "market-focused" producers relied on extensive use of local and international consultants and were well informed about major international market trends and what appealed to buyers in their market segments. Those that were actively promoting exports used the services of WOSA. On a local front, they emphasized their role in the respective wine route associations. They faced difficulties in keeping up with market demand for their product.

These firms paid particular attention to the selection of their foreign agents. They emphasized the importance of agents who understood their wine, valued its South African origin, and were able to exploit it effectively. For instance, a few years previously, one firm had relocated one of its directors to the United States to manage agent relationships. Some of the market-oriented producers had significantly increased the resources they committed to marketing. Their priority was media coverage and close relationships with agents or retail representatives in order to keep abreast of key developments.

By contrast, other established producers indicated that they "sell wherever they can" or "want to be in every market they can be in." They had mixed successes in their target markets and were either looking for new geographic markets or testing new segments. In part, this appears to have been in response to difficulties in selling all of their production. These firms did not emphasize the importance of their choice of agents or of managing those relationships closely.

In sum, there is a significant gap in performance within the established wine producers. The most distinctive differences occurred in regard to the introduction of new products at the upper end of the market and the consequent investments necessary in marketing and branding. The more successful established wineries were those that had greater resources available for innovation, because of strong direct consumer sales and equity investment. As a consequence, they could afford to hire external consultants, particularly for defining product strategy. Consulting expertise was viewed as essential because it gave producers confidence in their investment in innovation. The more successful established producers also worked more closely than their less successful peers with the industry institutions engaged in marketing. They were similarly more involved with the institutions that offered technical and research support and were likely to invest more heavily in vineyard improvements.

Financial strength, however, is only one dimension of their improved performance. A key deficiency in the weaker firms lay in the level of their marketing expertise. These firms had less understanding of concepts like market segmentation and product positioning and thus were unsure where to focus their innovation effort, particularly with regard to their product range. As a consequence, while these firms made significant investments to improve production, their returns were limited. By contrast, the firms that performed well had clear marketing strategies, made major innovations in marketing, and directly aligned all aspects of their production effort to coordinate with their marketing strategy.

Lessons Learned and Policy Implications

This study looked at three main influences on the wine industry over the past decade: the role of networks and associations; the role of strong policy incentives, such as the abolition of quotas and support to new wine growers, and institutions; and the need to innovate in response to domestic pressures and global changes. The industry has succeeded in improving bottled wines and substantially increasing export volumes, albeit from a low base.

There is wide disparity in performance between the different industry segments—and indeed considerable diversity within each industry segment. In the main, South African producers have been effective at innovation in product and production, for example, by introducing new varieties that are in demand, particularly in export markets, and in improving the quality of output. An under resourced but relatively effective network of technical support and research closely aligned to industry needs has aided these processes. The network is most intensively used by less well resourced producers, with better resourced producers more inclined to turn to the private sector for the required expertise, in the form of consulting viticulturalists and winemakers.

However, in comparison with other New World producers, growth in export value has been less impressive. South African producers have had limited success in exporting quality wines. The critical constraint on performance throughout the industry is not in the technical or research areas, not in production or in winemaking, but in marketing. The marketing constraint is being alleviated through the growing capacities of WOSA, an effective institution that has gained considerable legitimacy across the industry; by the rise of new brand-focused wine wholesalers that have developed close relations with producers; and by the increase in networking and sharing of knowledge about export markets among at least some local producers.

However, the impact of these developments has been uneven, especially in cooperatives. As a group, cooperatives are most obviously lacking in terms of marketing expertise. The cooperatives in the study have achieved limited success with brand development and with their marketing partnerships. The inadequate marketing capability of these high-volume producers, which account for a large share of total production, would appear to be a distinctive feature of the South African wine industry. Even so, some of these cooperatives have been able to launch their own brands, some of which have achieved international success.

Policy has been important. Each segment of the market has responded differently to policy incentives, perhaps owing to differences in their innovative capabilities and production history. For instance, some of the new producers face considerable challenges in the area of marketing, but financial constraints make advertising all but impossible despite reforms at the macro level. However, other new producers have responded innovatively to this reality, leveraging the high-quality products that are their primary asset. They have succeeded in creating awareness by garnering wine awards and high ratings, by producing very distinctive wines, by taking a personalized approach to marketing (sharing information on marketing channels), and by responding to consumer interest generated by Internet coverage. As a group, the new producers are more strongly export oriented than are established producers, in part because of their relatively weak positions in the domestic market and relatively unknown brands. Their contribution to the awareness of South African wines internationally may thus be disproportionate to their size.

What are the policy implications of the patterns of growth outlined above? A gauge to measure the strengthening of the South African wine industry is arguably the increase in the number and strength of the top South African wine brands. In this respect, further development of international brand management expertise among wholesalers and cooperatives is essential. In the main, these wine producers have not been able to effectively align the advances that they have made in production with the needs and requirements of their consumers. Instead, they have lagged behind the established and new producers.

While this is a subject for much discussion, it appears that policy to improve marketing mechanisms and provide marketing training to wine producers would have a very positive effect on the wine industry in South Africa.[5] Attention certainly must be paid to technical support and technological research, but the gains from further technological advances and innovations in the industry will depend critically on accompanying changes in marketing capabilities.

References

Wood, Eric, and David Kaplan. 2005. "Innovation and Performance Improvement in the South African Wine Industry." *International Journal of Technology and Globalization* 1 (3/4). Special Issue on Innovation, Clusters, and Systemic Learning in Developing Countries, edited by Banji Oyelaran-Oyeyinka and Rajah Rasiah.

---

5. In 2004, the University of Cape Town and the University of Adelaide established a joint executive management program aimed at developing business skills in the South African wine industry.

11

The Western Cape Textile and Clothing Cluster in South Africa

Rojit Sawkut

The South African clothing and textile industry is an established industry covering the entire value chain from fiber production to apparel manufacture. The industry is becoming increasingly focused on exports. Helping to stimulate growth are trade agreements with the European Union (Trade Development and Cooperation Agreement) and the United States (African Growth and Opportunities Act, AGOA).

The clothing sector accounts for 1.8 percent of overall employment in South Africa but 82 percent of the employment of semiskilled and unskilled labor. In July 2005 the National Bargaining Council for the Clothing Manufacturing Industry recorded that 89,608 people were directly employed in the sector, down by almost 9,000 from a year earlier. At its peak, employment in the clothing sector surpassed 170,000.[1] Exports, too, have fallen. In 2004, exports of apparel amounted to R338 million, constituting 19 percent of the apparel business. However, in 2003 exports of apparel had been 13.5 percent higher. The main factors that contributed to the drop in exports were the early impact of the phaseout of the Multifibre Arrangement (MFA) and the strength of the rand, which made exports less competitive in the world market.

In the early 1920s, the South African clothing sector was almost nonexistent. Clothing was either imported or tailored (October 1996). Real development occurred in the 1960s, when the sector almost doubled in size and changed its location. Before the 1960s, most of the industry was located in Johannesburg and Cape Town (Morris, Barnes, and Esselaar 2004). When apartheid limited the use of African labor in urban areas, the clothing industry moved to areas with concentrations of Indian and Colored labor—Durban, Cape Town, and areas bordering "bantustans"—the territories designated as tribal "homelands" for black South Africans and Namibians during the apartheid era.[2] Cape Town soon became the center of the South African clothing industry, because of the large retail chains based there (Gibbon 2002).

Today, the country's clothing sector is concentrated in the provinces of Western Cape, KwaZulu-Natal, and Gauteng (table 11.1). The number of clothing firms in

---

1. http://www.africanstatistics.co.za/Latest%20SA%20Sectors.htm#The_Textiles_and_Clothing_Industries
2. The term "bantustan," first used in the late 1940s, was coined from Bantu (meaning "people" in the Bantu languages) and -stan (meaning "land of" in the Persian language.

Table 11.1. *Clothing firms by province, 1990–2001*

Year	Western Cape	KwaZulu-Natal	Gauteng	OFS / Northern Cape	Total
1990	448	445	347	8	1248
1995	404	385	268	7	1064
1996	410	420	261	7	1098
1997	379	355	239	7	980
1998	361	301	226	6	894
1999	350	214	201	5	770
2000	351	186	179	6	722
2001	324	153	171	6	654
Growth of firms					
Annual percent 1990–5[3]	–1.97	–2.73	–4.98	–2.5	–3.08
Annual percent 1995–2001	–3.55	–13.55	–7.16	–2.38	–7.64

Source: Morris, Barnes, and Esselaar 2004.

each of the provinces has declined, particularly over the period 1995 to 2001, with KwaZulu-Natal experiencing the greatest proportional decline of 13.6 percent over the period. As of June 2004, according to the National Bargaining Council, there were a total of 827 clothing firms of which 327 were located in the Western Cape, 42 in the Eastern Cape, 219 in KwaZulu-Natal, and 239 in the Northern area.

More than half of the clothing employees represented by the National Bargaining Council are located in the Western Cape. Although employment in all provinces has declined, particularly since 1995, the decline in the Western Cape has been proportionally smaller than in other provinces, resulting in an increase in the proportion of clothing industry employees who work in the province. Based on these statistics, the Western Cape has both the largest number of firms and the highest employment level in the clothing sector. For this reason we selected it for deeper analysis.

Profile and Organization of the Cluster/Sector

The clothing industry in Western Cape Province has changed in the course of its significant growth over the last 70 years. The period from 1950 to 1980 was very important, with large increases in both the number of firms and the number of employees (table 11.2). In the 1990s, the number of firms increased, but employment fell. According to the National Bargaining Council, by June of 2004, the number of clothing firms in the Western Cape had fallen back to 327. This suggests a very important aspect of the clothing sector in the Western Cape—economies of scale were realized during the 1990s.

---

3. Note that the annual percentage growth has been calculated using the Compound Annual Growth Rate (CAGR). CAGR is not the actual return but rather an imaginary number that describes the rate at which the number of firms would have grown if at a steady rate over the years under consideration. The formula is CAGR = (ENDING VALUE/BEGINNING VALUE)$^{(1/\text{\# of years}) - 1}$

Table 11.2. *Western Cape clothing factories*

Year	Factories	Employees	Year	Factories	Employees
1935	30	3,500	1980	332	53,421
1940	40	4,772	1990	433	54,267
1950	104	13,204	1994	538	46,868
1960	166	19,787	2000	351	34,655
1970	253	37,743	2004	327	33,804

Source: Flaherty (2002), October (1996), and National Bargaining Council statistics.

The Western Cape clothing industry cluster contains a mix of firms of different sizes and levels of integration. Small firms, and cut, make, and trim firms (CMTs), mushroomed in the Western Cape during the last decade. October (1996) mentions the existence of "mini-clusters" of up to 100 small firms within the region. Such mini-clusters seem to consist of firms with similar specializations. Gibbon (2002) noted some interesting features among the Western Cape CMTs (box 11.1).

The Western Cape is central to the nation's textile, clothing, and leather industry. In 2001, nearly 35 percent of South Africa's total value added from textiles, clothing, and leather goods originated in the Western Cape (Morris, Barnes, and Esselaar 2004). By 2002, however, the value added by this sector in the Western Cape had declined by 4.2 percent. National Bargaining Council employment statistics by province show that more than half of all clothing employees represented by the council are located in the Western Cape. Although employment in all provinces in South Africa has declined since 1990, as noted, there has been a smaller percentage decline in the Western Cape, resulting in an increase in the proportion of clothing industry employees who work in this province (table 11.3).

The clothing firms in the Western Cape are concentrated in the Cape Town metropolitan area (Barnes 2005). The industry consists of full-line manufacturers as

Table 11.3. *Clothing industry employment by province, 1990–2001*

	Western Cape	KwaZulu-Natal	Gauteng	Eastern Province	OFS/ Northern Cape	Total	Western Cape as share of total
1990	54,564	44,623	16,092	3,118	2,711	121,108	45.1
1995	46,980	34,720	10,888	2,423	1,432	96,443	48.7
1998	41,874	26,397	8,994	1,793	1,262	80,320	52.1
1999	37,918	21,331	8,176	1,415	1,311	70,151	54.1
2000	38,262	19,714	7,517	1,489	1,004	67,986	56.3
2001	34,655	15,693	6,626	1,291	1,315	59,580	56.2
Employment growth (annual percent)							
1990–1995	−2.88	−4.58	−7.39	−4.68	−11.84	−4.31	
1995–2001	−4.85	−12.1	−7.91	−9.58	0.27	−7.61	

Source: Morris, Barnes, and Esselaar 2004.
Note: Data cover only employees represented by the National Bargaining Council.

Box 11.1. *"Cut, make, and trim" in the Western Cape*

At the end of the 1990s, so-called cut, make, and trim (CMT) firms producing for the domestic market constituted between a quarter and a half of all clothing firms in Western Cape, a considerably lower proportion than in Durban Metro, where they represented 320 out of 416 enterprises in 1998.

South Africa's CMT phenomenon emerged in three phases. In the 1960s and 1970s, when most large retailers began sourcing directly from manufacturers, some encouraged or helped set up CMT operations. In the 1970s, large manufacturers themselves started to use formal CMT firms to cope with production peaks, problematic styles, and shorter runs. Finally, in the 1990s, certain medium-size manufacturers began to specialize in cutting, finishing, design, merchandising, and marketing, transforming themselves into "design houses" while converting their technicians and machinists into formal or semiformal CMT workers, usually by providing technicians with plant on a leasehold basis. In a parallel process, informal CMT enterprises started to emerge following the outright closure of formal factories, as former employees spontaneously reemployed themselves in small and microenterprises. More recently, project-based informal clothing enterprises have emerged in African townships such as Khayelitsha and Mitchells Plain among groups without any previous background in the industry.

There are important gradations of scale and role in the Western Cape's CMT "sector." An elite of mostly European-owned CMT firms, with two or more sewing lines that can handle runs of up to 5,000 pieces, are fairly specialized in their product range. They serve the bigger chains, larger full manufacturers, and established design houses on a near-continuous basis. Those working for larger manufacturers sometimes act as additional sewing lines. Reputation—for quality and on-time delivery—is extremely important for maintaining continuity of business, which provides protection against insolvency in an industry that is very sensitive to wage costs.

Relations with customers tend to be highly regulated: negotiations on price take place on the basis of common assumptions concerning assembly minute-times and costs per minute, and payment is made within 48 hours of delivery. In some cases, elite CMT firms receive financial assistance from customers. But technology tends to be at least a generation out of date, working capital nonexistent, and there is no set route into full manufacture. Work-sharing between CMT firms is quite rare, although other forms of cooperation exist.

The next stratum of CMT firms are "jobbers" that work for smaller retail chains, less well established design houses, and the hawker market. The jobbers' output is relatively unspecialized. The racial profile of owners resembles more that of the Western Cape population generally. Maximum run lengths for this group tend to be no higher than 500 pieces, implying lower productivity. Traditionally, members of this stratum have not competed directly with the CMT elite, although this situation may be changing as average run lengths decline. As with the strata below them, continuity of production is rare, and firm casualty rates much higher than among the elite CMT firms. Machinery is mostly second-hand and often obsolete. Many companies function only between August and December, although within this period they may experience excess demand. Firms' financial problems are exacerbated by the fact that smaller chains are less good at pattern grading (implying higher minute times for manufacturing), at on-time component delivery, and at paying on time for work completed. Work sharing to deal with production peaks is more common among this stratum, and there is seasonal recourse to home workers.

The remaining strata of CMT firms are micro or small enterprises with varying degrees of sophistication. Some work under relatively stable conditions for boutiques, while others function artisanally, for example, making school and other uniforms on demand for local markets. Still others are cooperative-based enterprises operating on a survival basis, and often depending on local politicians to find them work. Corresponding to these differences are fundamental differences in quality of technology (industrial vs. domestic sewing machines) and design. Between these strata and the higher ones there is again no set upgrade.

There have been a number of politically driven initiatives to help micro and small CMT enterprises to gain the type of business available to the upper strata. Up to now these initiatives have tended to founder, mainly because of the small firms' deficits in quality and reliability.

Source: Gibbon 2002.

well as a large number of CMTs. In contrast, in KwaZulu-Natal the industry is composed mainly of CMTs. Western Cape firms face comparatively higher costs than firms in other regions. For example, "grade A" employees can earn R 611 per week in the Western Cape, but only R 463 in KwaZulu-Natal. Most of the firms concentrate on clothing for the higher end market, so the goods produced are of better quality. The firms are focused on the domestic market and the leading retailers based in this region. Most firms are South African owned.

A SWOT (strengths, weaknesses, opportunities, and threats) analysis presents a better picture of the Western Cape clothing sector (Box 11.2).

Box 11.2. *A SWOT Analysis of the Western Cape Clothing Sector*

Strengths

- Reliable telecommunications and public services reduce costs and shorten lead times.
- Firms are good at adhering to international labor and social standards.
- Utility costs are cheap compared with those of other countries.
- The industry enjoys some government support, such as the Duty Credit Certificate Scheme (DCCS).
- Firms in this region are closer to major export markets than firms in other provinces. Firms that presently make up the industry have already proven their capabilities by surviving the trade liberalization of the 1990s.
- The firms have well-established relationships with buyers in Western Europe and North America.

Weaknesses

- Many firms rely on weak currency to be competitive in the export markets. The volatility of the rand makes this a disadvantage.
- Labor rates and ancillary labor costs are high compared to other regions.
- Telecommunications and public services can be unreliable. The manufacturing process is inefficient.
- Employees lack training, and there are not enough trained people to replace those who retire.
- The industry has a negative attitude toward change, investment, and risk-taking.
- Clothing manufacturers have poor bargaining power with retailers.
- Locally obtained cotton is often of poor quality.

Opportunities

- Given that South Africa has higher costs, lower economies of scale, and longer lead times than its competitors, it should concentrate on products that have longer lead times and for which higher costs are acceptable. That is, South African firms should focus on better quality products for more specialized niche markets.
- South Africa should exploit middle-income markets such as Japan, the Middle East, Australia, the Russian Federation, and Asia, which are all experiencing massive increases in demand for apparel.
- Joining the Mercosur trade block in South America could help South Africa to tap the South American apparel market.
- The African export market could be more actively pursued through regional trade agreements, by organizations such as the South African Development Community (SADC).

Continued

> **Box 11.2.** *A SWOT Analysis of the Western Cape Clothing Sector—continued*
>
> *Opportunities—continued*
>
> - A proposed trade agreement between the South African Customs Union (SACU) and the United States would remove barriers to trade. Textiles and clothing are likely to be included. This agreement requires negotiation of new rules of origin, which may be more advantageous to the South African clothing industry than those contained in the AGOA agreement. South Africa will push for double transformation rules that would allow the use of imported yarn, provided the fabric is made in South Africa. There are still opportunities for export under AGOA, which has been extended to 2015. The stringent rules of origin contained in that agreement provide opportunities for the textile industry.
> - The development of a "Cape" or "South African" brand of clothing and fabrics with an African feel could help to increase exports.
>
> *Threats*
>
> - Global competition will increase owing to trade liberalization as the Multifibre Arrangement is phased out. China is a major threat.
> - Low-cost imports are a threat to local industry suppliers that compete with those imports in the domestic market.
> - Illegal imports and dumping are also a threat to local industry suppliers.
> - South Africa's inflexible labor market constrains formal employment growth and inhibits competitiveness.
> - The lack of design expertise in South Africa hurts the marketing of exports, as does the lack of innovation in both products and processes.
> - The lack of trust and cooperation between clothing producers and textile producers hinders the ability of firms to compete effectively. The rules of origin of various trade agreements increase the interdependence of these sectors of the industry, so it is extremely important for them to work together to improve the competitiveness of the industry as a whole.
>
> *Source:* Morris, Barnes, and Esselaar (2004).

Knowledge and Technology Aspects of the Industry/Cluster

External economies of scale are quite obvious in the Western Cape cluster.[4] Leading retailers have their headquarters in the Western Cape, firms have fairly reliable telecommunication and public services, firms are geographically well positioned, and they enjoy some government support. However, only a few firms in the Western Cape use technologically advanced methods of production. These firms welcome other firms to their plants to demonstrate the benefits of these methods. Western Cape clothing firms readily share information (October 1996). "All firms interviewed had visited other factories to look at new technology or different forms of work organization, such as just-in-time" (McCormick 1998, quoting October 1996).

Although firms learn from the experience of the others, and even visit other firms to see how new production techniques can reduce their costs and increase production, they still resist change. Morris, Barnes, and Esselaar (2004) concluded that the industry was unwilling to change, invest, and take risk—for that reason, technology spillovers had not taken place in this cluster. Reluctance to change is often found among small firms that are satisfied with what they are producing and

---

4. This part of the chapter has been adapted from McCormick (1998).

earning and do not seek to expand production. In today's era of globalization, however, if firms do not adapt to new technology and more advanced methods of productions, they are bound to fail and will have to leave the market.

The availability of computerized production and design packages has made it easier for willing firms to move up-market through change and training of workers. But iin the Western Cape, the use of computerized software to design, mark, and grade apparel is a phenomenon seen only in large and medium-sized firms. Small firms still use primitive techniques of production—a major reason why so many have closed. It should be understood, however, that specialized software calls for large investments in equipment and training.

To the best of our knowledge, no recent documentation clearly describes the skill levels of workers in the Western Cape and whether or not those levels have been increasing. Using figures for the skill levels of employees in the South African clothing sector as a whole as a proxy to estimate skill levels in the Western Cape (table 11.4), it appears that skill levels for employees have increased, but not significantly. There is a serious need to develop skills in the clothing and textiles industries.

The improvement of skills and cross-training of employees, management, and technical staffs will be necessary for firms to compete in international markets, especially after the phasing out of the MFA. However, Morris, Barnes, and Esselaar (2004) find that few new skilled people are entering the industry to replace those who leave, and that very little skills development is taking place within firms.

As in most developing countries, formal tertiary education in clothing and textiles is very limited in South Africa. Although a number of schools of design and fashion are found throughout the country, most offer courses at a very elementary level. They provide training to upgrade skills, which is important but insufficient. What is really required is a highly sophisticated technical school in design and fashion.

Until January 2001, only the Durban Technikon offered a course in textiles technology. Since then, the Peninsula Technikon in Cape Town has added a national diploma in textiles technology and reportedly plans to offer a bachelor of technology in the field. Nevertheless, both technikons are struggling to recruit enough students to make their courses viable. Therefore, to supplement educational opportunities at all levels, it appears that an awareness campaign is needed to generate enthusiasm for the potential of the South African clothing sector and the opportunities available for highly specialized workers.

In an attempt to develop and enlarge the skills base of employees in the textile and clothing, footwear, and leather industries, the South African government set up a sector education and training authority (SETA) for clothing, textiles, footwear

Table 11.4. *Proportion of employees with different skill levels (percent)*

Year	Highly skilled	Skilled	Semi- and unskilled
1990	3.4	12.6	83.9
1995	4.0	14.9	81.1
2004	4.4	13.1	82.5

Source: Computed from the DTI Statistics Newsletter, June 2005 (Annex 1), http://www.thedti. gov.za/stats/2_newsletterQ2.pdf.

and leather under the auspices of the Department of Labor. Thus far, the effectiveness of the CTFL SETA has been questionable. Research work undertaken through the Textiles Industry Development Council in early 2004 suggested that the SETA lacks credibility among manufacturers. Because many programs run through the SETA are not supported by the industry, they are ineffective. Ineffectiveness perpetuates the perception that the clothing and textile sector is not flourishing, and thus is to be avoided by bright youngsters and recent graduates.

Investment in capital and technology is another area in which the South African textile and clothing industry must improve to become more competitive. Morris, Barnes, and Esselaar (2004) found that from 1992 to 2000 the manufacturing sector spent an average of 5.8 percent of its sales revenues on new capital assets, compared to 3.8 percent in the textiles sector and just 1.4 percent in the clothing sector.[5] China, India, and Pakistan are spending intensively on new capital assets, while South Africa is lagging behind.

The same authors also noted that, in the Western Cape, retailers and manufacturers are often jointly involved in the design of garments for the local market. However, some large retailers, believing that manufacturers do not have adequate design and marketing skills, have performed design functions in-house, although there are indications that they would prefer not to have to do so.

The market for clothing is one of the most differentiated and stylized in the world. Customers are constantly asking for changes in designs, patterns, and quality. And the higher on the market scale a firm aims, the more it must invest in design. Morris, Barnes, and Esselaar (2004) note that Western Cape firms, which produce for the higher end of the domestic market, must improve their design and marketing skills if they wish to increase exports, especially high-end exports.

Policy and Incentives

Governments provide financial assistance to domestic firms as a means of promoting exports (export-led growth) and improving the country's balance of payments.[6] Export incentives include direct subsidies to lower export prices, tax concessions, credit facilities, and financial guarantees. Export incentives are often viewed as "unfair" trade practice by other countries frequently result in retaliatory action. The rules of the World Trade Organization call for such incentives to be replaced by other forms of assistance more compatible with the free trade objectives of the WTO. Such assistance programs would have the objective of increasing production capacity and productivity so that firms become more efficient and can compete on their own on the world trade market.

Export incentives in South Africa include export marketing and investment schemes, sector assistance schemes, export credit insurance, and export finance. A number of other supply-side measures also boost exports of various products. Two programs that directly affect the clothing sector are the Development Program

---

5. Capital investment in the textile sector should be higher than that in the clothing sector for two reasons: first, the textile sector is more capital-intensive than the clothing sector, and second, the textile sector still lags behind the clothing sector throughout Africa.
6. The section draws on the following Web sites http://www.mbendi.co.za/export/sa/export_incentives.htm, http://www.capegateway.gov.za/eng/yourgovernment/gsc/13416/services/11442/10163, and www.seardel.co.za/2004/chairmans_report.htm

for the Textile and Clothing Industry and Duty Credit Certificate Scheme. Both are described below.[7]

Development Program for the Textile and Clothing Industry. The program has as its objective the increased international competitiveness of the clothing sector. That objective was to be met through the phased reduction of ad valorem duties so as to reach certain end rates by September 2002. Minimum and maximum specific duties have been removed. Rebate items are to be withdrawn or phased out. Those items that are no longer in use will be withdrawn immediately. Exceptions include rebate provisions for export manufacturing 470.03 and the Duty Credit Certificate Scheme.

Duty Credit Certificate Scheme. The objective of the Duty Credit Certificate Scheme (DCCS) is to encourage textile and clothing manufacturers to compete internationally, independent of government subsidies. Under the scheme, the South African government extends to exporters of textiles and clothing "duty credit certificates" that compensate exporters for a certain amount of the duties they must pay on imports of certain textile and clothing products. Benefits are granted subject to participation in the Performance Measurement Program (PMP) and the achievement of certain performance, training, and export targets. The PMP is administered by the National Productivity Institute on behalf of the Department of Trade and Industry.

Regional Industrial Development Program (RIDP). The Regional Industrial Development Program (RIDP) of the 1980s was designed to promote industry in rural areas. Clothing sector employment in the included areas increased to about 30 percent toward the end of the RIDP. There was also a significant level of new foreign investment during this period, primarily by Taiwanese firms. The firms were located in the Bantustans and in lower-wage larger regional centers, such as Newcastle and Kimberley. When the RIDP subsidies, most South African firms relocated to urban areas, while the foreign-owned firms remained where they were first located and increased in number.

Finance for Textiles, Clothing, Leather, and Footwear. The objective of this program is to provide financial assistance to textile and clothing firms so that the firms can develop and expand. Loans of R 500,000 or more are offered with interest rates linked to the prime rate. Grants and rebates are also available.

Istanbul Declaration. CloTrade and TexFed are two federations that represent clothing and textile workers in South Africa. Both have signed the Istanbul Declaration, through which textile and clothing employers in many countries requested a three-year delay in the dismantling of quotas on textile and clothing exports from China following the expiration of the MFA.

Textile and Clothing Industry Development Council (TCDC). This body provides a platform for government, the Textile Federation (TexFed), and the clothing industry to share views about the clothing industry and to discuss and jointly develop sustainable strategies for the clothing and textile industries.

Clothing Benchmarking and Cluster Development Initiatives. The initiatives are a joint venture between the Western Cape provincial government and regional clothing manufacturers. The objective of the partnership is to counter the threats confronting the clothing industry and to maximize its opportunities. Activities include the

---

7. More details on these programs are available at http://www.mbendi.co.za/export/sa/export_incentives.htm.

benchmarking of firms within the sector, the design of strategies to enhance the competitiveness of firms, and the promotion of strategic collaboration within the industry.

Clothing and Textile Services Center (Clotex). The clothing and textile industry is supported by the Department of Economic Development and Tourism through the Clothing and Textile Services Center (Clotex). Clotex provides training programs to boost labor productivity, financial skills, and computer skills, as well as raise access to information, legal advice, and technology. With government funds, Clotex has organized a clothing and textile exhibition, a mentoring and linkages project, and training for CMT employees. Current training includes garment construction, pattern making, and design.

Key Success Factors

The Western Cape clothing and textile industry flourished during the 1990s, but since 1995 changes in the international market have caused a decline in the number of firms and the level of employment. Nevertheless, in the Western Cape the sector remains as important today as it was in the 1990s. Many factors have contributed to the success of the clothing sector in the province.

A key contributor to success has been that in the Western Cape, clothing manufacturers grouped together for their mutual benefit. The two largest clothing manufacturers' organizations are the Cape Clothing Manufacturers Association, which represents mainly the large and established manufacturers, and the Garment Manufacturers Association, which represents small firms such as CMTs.

There are also some small manufacturers' associations, for instance, the CMT Employers' Association and Mitchells Plain Garment Manufacturers Association. The benefits of being associated are numerous. Among these are cooperation to handle large orders, the sharing of information, the ability to reduce costs by sharing marketing agents, the sharing of machinery, specialization, and the subcontracting of orders.

A number of government and institutional initiatives have enhanced productivity in the Western Cape area. The apartheid-era Regional Industrial Development Program (RIDP) offered substantial five-year subsidy packages to firms located anywhere outside the Johannesburg, Pretoria, and Durban areas. As a consequence, firms were established in or relocated to the Western Cape. Until January 2005, South African exports did not fall under the MFA quota restrictions. Today, AGOA continues to offer opportunities for export to the U.S. market free of duty and quotas.

In 2004, with support from the German Agency for Technical Cooperation, a team from the Technology Station in Clothing and Textiles at the Peninsula Technikon conducted an appraisal of innovation processes in the the clothing and textile value chain in the Western Cape using the RALIS method developed by the German firm, Mesopartner.[8] The team reported the following key success factors in the clothing and textile sector in the Western Cape (TSCT 2004).

---

8. Rapid Appraisal of Local Innovation Systems (RALIS) diagnoses the strengths and weaknesses of the local innovation system, provides participants with an opportunity to engage directly with key actors in the local innovation system, and generates a set of proposals for practical activities to strengthen the local innovation system. http://www.mesopartner .com/englisch/e-ralis.html.

- A positive attitude toward the future
- Continuous holistic training (with CEOs personally involved as trainers)
- Engagement in niche markets (at least in part)
- Active involvement in product and process innovation (mostly in cooperation with customers and suppliers)
- Annual capital investments to keep production and processing capacities technologically up to date
- Incentive schemes to raise workforce productivity
- Strategic, intimate customer relationships.

Lessons Learned and Policy Implications

Clothing firms in the Western Cape will not be able to survive globalization without support from government institutions. With the MFA phase-out, the international competitiveness of firms in the Western Cape has decreased in favor of giants such as China, India, and Bangladesh. However, Western Cape producers are grouped together under various producers' associations and are willing to work together to overcome the challenges they face. In fact, they have already proved themselves, as they survived the trade liberalization of the 1990s. The provincial government should devise strategies to support clothing firms in the Western Cape, seeking assistance at the national level where needed. Some strategies that the provincial government might adopt:

- Reduce red tape and bureaucracy in the process of exporting clothing products. A one-stop shop for all formalities is needed.
- Provide training facilities to improve, retrain, and cross-train workers in the sector to enhance productivity.
- Establish schools of design so that enthusiastic designers and stylists can be educated and made available to the clothing industry. These designers could help the industry become more upscale, while perhaps creating a niche market for a South African or Western Cape brand.
- Establish programs to teach clothing and textile industry skills, so that trained graduates are readily available to firms.
- Provide financial support to firms so that they can reorganize and modernize their plants, adding technologically advanced equipment and production techniques.
- Commission studies of the needs and concerns of producers, and take action consistent with the findings of those studies.
- Conduct continuous benchmarking.
- Organize fashion shows in the Cape Town district, inviting international buyers and the fashion press.
- Arrange for freight discounts for firms exporting more than a certain quantity of containers per year. Freight charges are too high for Western Cape producers.
- Work out strategies to reduce energy costs for clothing producers.
- Create institutions to help Western Cape producers make contacts international clients.
- Work with firms to inform them of the opportunities available to them, such as the export incentives available under AGOA.

References

Barnes, J. 2005. "A Strategic Assessment of the South African Wearing Apparel Sector." Report originally prepared for Trade and Industrial Policy Strategies and presented at the National Economic Development and Labour Council (NEDLAC), SATPP Policy Dialogue Workshop, Johannesburg. www.tips.org.za/events/satppjuly2005.asp

Flaherty, D. 2002. "Locational Inertia in South African Clothing Firms", Department of Economics, University of Massachusetts. www.commerce.uct.ac.za/DPRU/flaherty.pdf

Gibbon, P. 2002. "South Africa and the Global Commodity Chain for Clothing: Export Performance and Constraints." Centre for Development Research (CDR) Working Paper, Vol. 2, Num. 7, Month (2).

McCormick D. 1998. "Enterprise Clusters in Africa: On the Way to Industrialization?" IDS Discussion Paper 366, University of Nairobi.

Morris, M., J. Barnes, and J. Esselaar. 2004. "An Identification of Strategic Interventions at the Provincial Government Level to Secure the Growth and Development of the Western Cape Clothing and Textiles Industries." Compiled for the WCPG Department of Economic Development and Tourism.

October, L. 1996. "Sectors, Clusters and Regions: A Study of Cape Clothing Industry." DPRU Working Paper 2, University of Cape Town.

TSCT (Technology Station in Clothing and Textiles). 2004. "Observations and Results from RALIS Exercise Conducted in the Clothing and Textile Sector Conducted in the Western Cape, South Africa." Unpublished paper prepared by the Technology Station in Clothing and Textiles of Peninsula Technikon, Cape Town.